you need to be free. Vicki's message is an invitation to walk in peace and wonder and real joy amid the daily demands that surround you."

—SUSIE DAVIS
AUTHOR, *UNAFRAID*

"Vicki is winsome and gentle as she leads us toward greater freedom and more of God. Her writing feels like our coffee dates—warm and sincere and deeply committed to God's glory and our good."

—JENNIE ALLEN
IF:GATHERING FOUNDER AND AUTHOR, *RESTLESS*

"Well, she's done it again! Another incredibly well-written book at just the right time. Vicki continues to amaze me with her ability to drill down to bedrock on important issues that all of us struggle with in one way or another. Those of us who are always blowing and going from one thing to the next will find Vicki's book helpful in so many ways. Don't wait another minute before you read it so that God can restore your body, soul, and spirit."

—DR. CHRIS THURMAN
PSYCHOLOGIST AND BESTSELLING AUTHOR, *THE LIES WE BELIEVE*

"Busyness leads to barrenness, emotionally and spiritually. *Rest Assured* is a wonderful rest stop for much-needed soul care. Thank you, Vicki, for boldly exposing our chronic partial attention!"

—JACKIE KENDALL
BESTSELLING AUTHOR, *LADY IN WAITING*

"*Rest Assured* is such a timely guide for this generation of busy women (present company included). As I read it, my soul resonated like a tuning fork, singing out, 'Yes, yes, I need this type of rest!' Vicki helps us discover the truth, desire, and tools necessary for seeking God and His supernatural transforming rest for our weary souls. Then we can fulfill the call of God on our lives and enjoy them too. I plan to buy a box of *Rest Assured* and pass them out to every busy mom I know!"

—TAMI OVERHAUSER
BLOGGER AND BUSY MOM OF FOUR

"Vicki Courtney has bravely taken on an all too common malady in our Christian culture—soul exhaustion. In *Rest Assured: A Recovery Plan for Weary Souls*, she explores the reasons so many of us fall into this trap, as well as offers creative and long-term plans to avoid it in the future. Her questions at the end of each chapter and her One Week Dares prod the reader into seriously considering lifestyle changes that will lead to refreshment rather than fatigue. There is an art to tending to our souls. Thank you, Vicki, for showing us how to do just that."

—SUSIE HAWKINS
AUTHOR, *FROM ONE MINISTRY WIFE TO ANOTHER*

"*Rest Assured* is a much-needed book in our culture, which rushes without taking time to really live. Vicki reminds us how to be still and enjoy the greater part of walking with Jesus. I will be recommending this book every chance I get!"

—ESTHER BURROUGHS
NATIONAL SPEAKER

"*Rest* is a four-letter word that most women I know simply can't fit into their lives because they are too *busy* (another four-letter word). I love how Vicki helps identify what is keeping us from rest and time with Jesus and then encourages us to make changes and even offers one-week dares to be different. I think this speaks to every woman out there, no matter what stage of life she is in."

—KELLY STAMPS
WOMEN'S COUNCIL AT FBC BENTONVILLE AND BLOGGER

"After reading the first few pages of chapter 1, I did not want to put *Rest Assured* down. It was as though Vicki had insight into my life. From a former 'weary soul,' thank you, Vicki, for allowing God to use you to speak truth into my life and the lives of many, many women. Jeremiah 6:16 has new meaning for me."

—BETTY A. STOOKSBURY
ALASKA CHRISTIAN WOMEN'S MINISTRY DIRECTOR

Praise for Rest Assured

"The moment I met Vicki Courtney will stick out in my mind forever. We were in a bathroom at a retreat, and somehow, amid soapy hands and paper towels, we saw deep into each other's soul. She saw my weariness, and I saw her wisdom, and in that moment she promised to come alongside if I ever needed it. The truth is, we all need it. We all need a hand of wisdom to speak life and encourage deep rest that can be found only in Christ. In *Rest Assured* Vicki holds out her hand in invitation to journey together toward lasting rest and hope in Christ. Honest, authentic, and admittedly still in process, Vicki has exactly the kind of hand I am grateful to hold."

—Logan Wolfram
Allume executive director and host,
speaker, and author, *Curious Faith*

"If you're tired, stressed, overworked, or maybe even a little bit shaky with boundaries (I'm raising my hand), this book will do your heart and mind a world of good. In *Rest Assured* Vicki Courtney addresses the epidemic of busyness in our try-hard culture, and she candidly shares her own struggles as she digs deep into this issue. True to form, her words are comforting, grounded in Scripture, and relatable to the core. As she lovingly redirects us to Sabbath and rest, Vicki helps us examine our motives and reflect on our choices—and she dares us to make practical changes. The result is a book that's like a dear friend who loves you enough to say, 'I get it. Life is hectic. But you're made for more.'

"For me, *Rest Assured* has been the perfect book at the perfect time, an antidote for my particular brand of overcommitted crazy. It's a balm for weariness that has challenged me to ask and answer some difficult questions, and I can honestly say that I'm better for having read it. I'm confident that you will be too."

—Sophie Hudson
Author, *Home Is Where My People Are* and
A Little Salty to Cut the Sweet

"How my soul needed this book. And yours does too. Vicki falls on her own sword with transparency and humility, opening your eyes to what your soul is thirsty for, even providing the rest stops to drink of it."

—Dannah Gresh
Bestselling author, *And the Bride Wore White*

"This book is an invitation—an invitation to be human. I adore books that sit with me on the couch and offer permission to be the struggler that I am. It is here that Vicki Courtney sits down next to me in her living room, holds my hand as I weep through exhaustion and shallow relationships, and looks me in the eye with the truth of intimacy that offers peace to my weary bones. As an overcommitted wife, mom, and dreamer, who prefers earning over engaging any day of the week, every pore on my skin ached for the tender truths found in this book. Thank you, Vicki, for loving us enough to prick our souls for the most precious commodity—our time— and for giving us a road map back to the brave place of rest we have been craving all along. I loved this book to the depths."

—Kasey Van Norman
Bestselling author, *Named by God* and *Raw Faith*

"Vicki Courtney is one of my favorite authors to read because she has so much wisdom to offer. Reading her books is like having a conversation with your smart, older sister who has been there, done that, and lived to tell about it. In Vicki's new book, *Rest Assured*, she outlines the importance of giving our souls time to rest, and I felt myself taking a deep breath as I read her words. If you feel like you're stressed, too busy, and just looking for some peace in the midst of a crazy, busy world, then I can't encourage you enough to open up the pages of this book and take in all Vicki has to say about finding a fix for your weary soul."

—Melanie Shankle
New York Times bestselling author, *Nobody's Cuter Than You*

"Is your overbooked calendar bossing you and your family around? Is your schedule making demands of your soul that keep you from truly enjoying your life? Then rest assured you're holding the encouragement

"Vicki communicates with timely, transparent authenticity in sharing a woman's everyday struggles. Her life challenges are as real as mine. This book encourages Christian women to have rest in Christ through the disciplined study of His Word. Her writings instruct us to take our contentment in Jesus to another level."

—JULIE STEWART
MOTHER OF THREE, NOBTS PROFESSOR'S WIFE, WOMEN'S
MINISTRY DIRECTOR, AND EVENT COORDINATOR

"In much the same way Richard Fosters' book *Freedom of Simplicity* and Richard Swenson's book *Margin* aroused within my soul the desire to scale back and seek first God's kingdom in all things and in every decision to see margin in my daily life, Vicki's book *Rest Assured* gave me the necessary tools to actually take the steps to free my tethered soul and release me to enjoy the *now*. I look forward to implementing her tools in my daily life in the weeks and months ahead. This book is both life-altering and extremely practical. A must-read for every busy mom and busy woman wondering how to find balance in a world screaming for our attention every waking moment."

—ASHLEY SMITH
FORMER GIRLS' MINISTRY LEADER AND BIBLE STUDY LEADER,
FIRST BAPTIST CHURCH, HENDERSONVILLE, TENNESSEE

"As a serial performer and overachiever, I frequently ask myself, *How did I get here? What am I trying to prove? Why am I so tired?* Vicki provides biblical truth and practical steps that give you permission to finally stop needlessly striving and embrace rest for your burnt-out soul."

—ASHLEY ANDERSON
AREA DIRECTOR, YOUNG LIFE COLLEGE,
UNIVERSITY OF TEXAS AT AUSTIN

REST ASSURED

REST ASSURED

A Recovery Plan for Weary Souls

Vicki Courtney

W Publishing Group

An Imprint of Thomas Nelson

Published in Nashville, Tennessee, by W Publishing Group, an imprint of Thomas Nelson.

Thomas Nelson titles may be purchased in bulk for educational, business, fund-raising, or sales promotional use. For information, please e-mail SpecialMarkets@ThomasNelson.com.

Library of Congress Cataloging-in-Publication Data

Courtney, Vicki.
   Rest assured: a recovery plan for weary souls / Vicki Courtney.
      pages cm
   Includes bibliographical references.
   ISBN 978-0-8499-6492-3 (trade paper)
   1. Christian women—Religious life. 2. Rest—Religious aspects—Christianity. I. Title.
BV4527.C6885 2015
248.8'43—dc23

2015014684

Printed in the United States of America

15 16 17 18 19 20 RRD 6 5 4 3 2 1

Contents

Introduction

I arise in the morning torn between a desire to improve
(or save) the world and a desire to enjoy (or savor)
the world. This makes it hard to plan the day.

—E. B. WHITE

It's been several years, but I still remember the question that interrupted my life and set me on a course to discover rest for my weary soul. I was at a retreat with about fifty other women, most of whom served in ministry. We had broken up into small groups and were given the task of answering one simple question: *What is your greatest risk?* Most of the women in my group were in their twenties and thirties and smack-dab in the exhausting chapter of life where they were juggling the demands of marriage, parenting, and part-time or full-time work, as well as their respective ministries. The retreat offered a safe place to resurrect long-forgotten dreams that had been buried under a heap of everyday duties and obligations.

"I always thought we would adopt a child, but now that we have three children of our own, we're too worn-out to entertain the thought," shared one woman. "Maybe that's what we're supposed to do. I guess that would be my greatest risk." Another woman shared, "I would write a book. It's been a lifelong dream, but it's a risk because I'm not sure I could handle the rejection if a publisher didn't pick it up. And it's not like I really have time." And another shared, "I've always wanted to minister to families who have lost a loved one to cancer. That's my story, but I have so much on my plate as it is."

The risks shared were raw and vulnerable, seasoned with wistful mights, maybes, and somedays. I couldn't help but notice the dreams seemed to be rooted in activity or service, yet the women all admitted to already feeling overwhelmed. And then it was my turn. I had been in their shoes at one point, burdened with a desire to follow a dream, change the world, or quite simply make a small difference in someone's life. If I had been asked the question twenty years earlier, I would have chimed in with the same urgent passion and shared that my greatest risk was to start a ministry that would encourage girls and women to see themselves through the eyes of God rather than the eyes of the world. I had experienced this battle firsthand and petitioned God as a young believer to allow me to share my story for His kingdom purposes. God took me up on the offer, and I had witnessed my greatest risk become a reality. It resulted in a full calendar of speaking engagements for a solid fifteen years, dozens of books and Bible studies, a national ministry with a staff of six (at its height), all, of course, while juggling the standard duties that came with being a wife and mother to three children.

To this day, I consider that risk one of the most exciting adventures of my life. Yet it didn't come without a price. After years spent trying to maintain a pace that left little margin for rest, I found myself worn-out and exhausted. My zeal was gone, my passion extinguished, my soul desperately empty. And this was the place I found myself several years ago that day at the retreat. As I thought about the question, "What is your greatest risk?" I realized that my greatest risk at that moment was not to do more, serve more, or prove more, but rather to do *less*. Much less. So I decided to tell the truth. "My greatest risk is slowing down and resting. I have forgotten how to be still." It had been a burden on my heart for years, but I'd always stopped short of openly confessing it. Until then.

After I shared my risk, several women approached me and confessed that they, too, were feeling weary and worn-out on the majority of days. They were over-connected, over-burdened with worries, and searching for something more. One woman shared that she was plagued with a nagging sense that no matter how much she did, it was never enough.

As I drove home from the retreat, I thought about the word *enough* and the pressure so many Christian women feel to achieve enough. In the months that followed I encountered women at speaking events who echoed the same confessions of feeling weary over trying to be enough in every area of their lives. Enough in their marriages. Enough as mothers. Enough in their jobs. Enough in their churches. Enough in their children's schools. Enough to their friends and neighbors. Enough on social media. Enough to the needy and less fortunate. Enough in their relationships with God. Enough, already! No wonder we're worn out and our souls lack rest. God alone is the never-ending source of *enough*, so why do we wear ourselves out trying to find it elsewhere?

The retreat was a wake-up call that set me on a course to discover rest for my weary soul. I still have a long way to go, and oftentimes it feels like my progress is two steps forward and one step back. In fact, I suffered a relapse while writing this book. In my despair I confessed the relapse to my editor, and she said something that gave me the courage to continue: "Vicki, write from that place of honesty." She went on to confide that she, too, was in the overcommitted, I'm-in-over-my-head-and-tired-of-being-tired all-too-familiar place in which women like us commonly find ourselves. I love my editor. Honestly, she's become more than just an editor to me. She is a kindred spirit, a friend, and, most importantly, a sister in Christ who is not afraid to admit that sometimes, behind her sweet smile and calm demeanor, she, too, is just limping along in this journey of faith. Just like you. Just like me. She ended our conversation by asking if she could pray for us both. In desperation we sought comfort at the throne of grace.

I want you to know that I wrote this book from that place of heartfelt desperation rather than one of victorious accomplishment. I wrote this book for myself as a prescription to the unrest in my own hurried soul. And if my hunch is correct, you are also in that same desperate place and in need of a prescription.

The Good Way

When God called me into the ministry in 1998, He led me to a specific verse as a foundation for my ministry.

The verse is Jeremiah 6:16:

> This is what the LORD says:
> "Stand at the crossroads and look;
>   ask for the ancient paths,
>   ask where the good way is, and walk in it,
>   and you will find rest for your souls." (NIV)

This verse paints a realistic picture of where we stand at this very moment. That is, if we can slow down long enough to ponder the choice before us. Leaving our familiar path will require that we change directions. This will not be an easy task. The "good way" is not a popular path, and most Christians will fall into step with the world, never questioning the pace nor stopping to consider if they are even on the right road. Ignorantly, they will assume it is the good way by the sheer fact that the world has deemed it so.

When God advised the fickle Israelites to "stand at the crossroads" and choose the good way, they refused. The passage in Jeremiah 6:16 ends with this phrase: "But you said, 'We will not walk in it.'" I find it unbelievable that they would trade rest in their souls for the same old dreaded path they had been on previously (one that can best be summed up by their penchant for false idols in a frantic search for satisfaction). Yet are you and I any different? God points us in the right direction, but we stubbornly refuse to change course.

This book is not intended to be a quick fix or a one-time cure-all, so I want to remove that pressure on the front end. My prayer is that this book will produce in each of us an awareness so that when we find ourselves scrambling down the same weary path once again (and trust me; it's only a matter of time), we can catch ourselves. The truth is most of us will spend our entire lives learning and relearning what it is to be still. My hope is that once we've tasted the benefits of being still, we won't tarry long on the same path that leaves us feeling overcommitted, overwhelmed, and over-connected and, as a result, robs our souls of rest.

How to Use This Book

I have divided the book into two parts to make the journey as simple as possible. Part One is an intervention and highlights four common enemies of rest. In Part Two, I introduce a recovery plan and offer a "One-Week Dare" at the end of each chapter to help put the principles into practice in our everyday lives. Participation is optional but highly encouraged. I have also included questions at the end of each chapter to help you dig deeper, whether you read the book alone or in a group setting. If you are going through the book with a group, consider devoting a week to each of the chapters in Part One and to each of the chapters in Part Two (for a total of eight weeks). However, if that is not possible, I encourage you to combine the chapters in Part One into fewer weeks to allow a full week per chapter in Part Two and fully exercise the One-Week Dares.

Finally, I have included a bonus guide for a Thirty-Day Restoration to be done upon completion of the book (apart from the group). It is entirely optional and offers an overview of material in the book to further solidify the principles and biblical truths. Ideally, it would be good to reconnect as a group at the end of the Thirty-Day Restoration period for the purpose of celebration. Have the women share what God taught them through the book. You might even encourage the women to pair up with a buddy and check in on one another from time to time to make sure they are staying the course.

The Invitation

In Matthew 11, Jesus issued an invitation: "Come to me, all who labor and are heavy laden, and I will give you rest. Take my yoke upon you, and learn from me, for I am gentle and lowly in heart, and you will find rest for your souls. For my yoke is easy, and my burden is light" (Matt. 11:28–30). One Bible commentary notes,

"Rest for the soul is the most desirable rest; to have the soul to dwell at ease."[1]

That is my deepest desire—to have a soul that dwells at ease. Consider this book a road map to guide us to that place, a road map that will lead us back to our Savior.

So what do you say? Are you longing for rest in your soul? The good way awaits. I can't promise you the journey will be easy, but I can promise you it will be worth it. Of that, you can rest assured.

PART I

ENEMIES OF REST

The Intervention

The Badge of Busyness

"I'm on my way, sweetie." Pat brushed by me in a flurry as she delivered a tray of food to a nearby table at my favorite diner. The diner sits in the middle of a small town where we own a weekend home, about an hour away from the hustle and bustle of the big city. I come here to write, think, and slow down. Folks don't typically move fast in this little hamlet. Except for Pat, that is. If you caught her during the morning rush, you would witness an impressive feat of multitasking. As she zigzagged from one table to the next, her movements reminded me of the Road Runner, who made a full-time job of staying one step ahead of Wile E. Coyote in the classic cartoons from yesteryear's Saturday mornings.

After refilling about a half dozen coffee cups, Pat appeared at my side with her order pad ready. "What'll you have, sweetie?"

I answered quickly, "I'll have two eggs over medium, wheat toast, and grits—no bacon." I'd learned not to hesitate. If Pat began to tap her pencil nervously on the order pad, you knew you had about five seconds to spit it out, or she'd dart off to another task, offering a polite, "I'll be back when you're ready, honey."

As she finished jotting down my order, the bell over the front door clanged its high-pitched tone, signaling another new customer's arrival. Pat politely barked over her shoulder, "Seat yourself, sweetie. I'm on my way." And off she went. She didn't have a spare second to indulge in idle chitchat. Pat did the work of four people, so there was no reason for me to take it personally. No one did.

While I sipped on my coffee, I thought about Pat's familiar mantra, "I'm on my way." In many respects it summed up the bulk of my adult years. I was *always* "on my way," busily bouncing from one activity to another, never quite feeling I had the time to unpack a bag, kick off my shoes, and stay awhile—to enjoy the moment. I barely had time to catch my breath before another obligation, duty, person, deadline, or task beckoned and demanded my undivided (ha!) attention. I blamed my calendar for the frenzy, as if it were a silent master holding a whip, giving me no choice but to obey its schedule. In my own defense, I attempted to slow down along the way, recalling the countless sermons I'd heard about rest and keeping the Sabbath. But my bold declarations were always short-lived. Before long I'd rev back up to my frenetic speed, with no rest and no space to breathe.

As I reflected on my tendencies, I realized that something deep within my being was compelling me to maintain the breakneck pace. *Something* drove me to fill every brief pause or empty hour with more activities and commitments. I desperately wanted to put my foot on the brakes and exit the fast lane, but I couldn't bring myself to actually stop the frenzy. I *hated* the pace, but at the same time, I *needed* it. I *complained* about it in one breath and *bragged* about it in the next. Maybe that should have been my first clue that something was terribly broken in my soul. I longed to be free from the busyness that enslaved me, but failed to realize *I* was the taskmaster holding the whip—not my calendar. I alone held the keys to the chains that bound me.

Crazy Busy and Proud of It

Ask someone the simple question, "How are you?" and you'll probably hear phrases like "super busy," "swamped," "overwhelmed," and "wish there were more hours in the day." As a bonus you might even get a play-by-play rundown of the overbooked calendar, spoken, of course, in an exasperated tone with a heavy sigh. Trust me, I'm stepping on my own toes here. I've been this person, and I wish I could go back and slap her silly. My rehearsed speech sounded a little like this: "Life is pretty crazy right now. I've got a full speaking calendar this fall, a list of writing deadlines I probably won't make, the kids' ballgames and activities that take up my weekends, and I just volunteered to help chair the silent auction at the kids' school." Looking off into the distance with a wistful gleam in my eye, I might have even added a wishful, "I look forward to a day when things slow down," or "I'd give anything to be bored."

I spoke about my life as if I had absolutely no control over the crazy pace, as if some invisible drill sergeant dictated my calendar and made sure every spare moment was productive and useful. My recounting of the pace of my life might have sounded like a woeful complaint, but something else was camouflaged underneath: a slight ring of pride. My frenzied, overbooked calendar was becoming the silent proof to others, and to myself, that my life was full and important. Somewhere along the way, busyness had become the barometer for measuring my worth and value. The busier I was, the more I mattered, or at least that's how I felt.

I am a writer and speaker, and though that doesn't demand that I clock in at an office Monday through Friday, it is a full-time job with requirements that often go beyond the normal boundaries of a forty-hour week. At the height of my busyness, I would make bold declarations about how I would force myself to slow down. *After* I finished a season of speaking engagements. *After* I met a book deadline. *After* my kids wrapped up a hectic school year. Yet when *after* finally arrived, I was off and running again in another leg of the race. In spite of my determination to create a less stressful calendar, my success was always short-lived because when empty blocks of time appeared, I couldn't seem to make peace with them. I struggled to adjust to a slower, more relaxed pace. Whether it was related to my career or my home life, I could *always* squeeze in one more thing—for me it might be one more speaking engagement, writing deadline, volunteer opportunity, or activity for the children. When I wasn't busy, I felt restless and ill at ease. When I was busy, I felt weary and in need of rest. It was a never-ending, vicious cycle.

Not all forms of busyness are unhealthy. Not all well-filled calendars are toxic. Many people experience bouts of seasonal busyness that are an exception to an otherwise well-balanced pace of life. However, a season of frenzy can turn into a lifestyle of chaos unless you make a concerted effort to guard your calendar. Has your brand of busyness lapsed into the unhealthy realm of chronic busyness?

Take a look at the following list to evaluate your risk for chronic busyness.

You might be too busy if:

- You struggle to say no when asked to do something, even when you know you don't have time to add anything else to your plate.
- You operate at a hurried pace throughout your entire day.
- You have a hard time leaving your work behind, and it often bleeds over into your home life.
- You get impatient when things don't move along as quickly as you'd like.
- You feel panicked when unexpected situations threaten to wreck your well-planned day because you have little wiggle room in your schedule.
- You don't easily settle down and relax. Even in rare moments when you are still, your mind is engaged and racing.
- You are short-tempered with your family members, quickly snapping at them when the day's events don't seem to click along as planned. (And they rarely do!)
- You have little downtime, and you don't make an effort to schedule it daily or weekly.
- You feel rushed in your alone time with God; spending time with Him moves to the bottom of the priority list if your day is too crowded.
- You find little time to pursue your hobbies and interests because leisure is a luxury, not a requirement.
- You feel guilty when engaging in a relaxing activity (e.g., thumbing through a magazine, watching a favorite TV show, lingering over lunch with a friend).
- Your lack peace in your soul.

How did you do? Most of us have lapsed into an unrealistic pace over time and have told ourselves that little can be done about it. We have been duped by an American culture that demands a frenzied pace as the norm. And in our rush we never slow down long enough to ponder whether God has endorsed this ludicrous pace.

Beneath the Busyness

Why is it hard for so many of us to establish a moderate pace in our lives? If we sincerely want to find relief, we must be willing to take a deeper look at the root of the problem. Whether our busyness is related to our careers, our home lives, or a combination of both, what is going on beneath the surface? I don't want to oversimplify the problem, but I believe that somewhere along the way, we were lured into a pattern of chronic busyness by a payoff. Busyness = Reward.

Which of the following payoffs have lured you into the destructive cycle of chronic busyness?

Payoff #1: Satisfaction.

Many of us recognize cognitively that satisfaction can be found in God alone, but our actions demonstrate that such truth has not traveled from our heads to our hearts. Like junkies in need of a fix, we chase one false god after another in a desperate attempt to satisfy our hungry souls.

If you have been scammed by this particular payoff, another telltale symptom of your situation might be the sporadic amount of time you spend with God. In short, if your schedule gets crazy, He's usually the first one to get the boot. He might receive a brief nod by reading an online devotional, but that drive-by won't deliver the kind of satisfaction your soul truly craves. Like eating a candy bar for lunch, your stomach feels good for a minute, but you'll be craving more substance in no time.

The ironic but sad truth surrounding misplaced satisfaction is that even if we reach our ultimate end goals (a nicer home, a promotion at the office, a child who makes the honor roll; you fill in the blank: _____), our pursuits will not provide us with lasting contentment. We'll get a temporary buzz, but nothing more. Just look back at the history of our Israelite friends in the Old Testament. Their incessant habit of looking to worldly idols failed to deliver—every time. After the buzz wore off, they were left with more unrest in their souls. Sound familiar?

Think about it. If we are too busy to spend time with God on a consistent basis, we are too busy. Period. And if we are able to make time for the things we deem important, and God doesn't top the list, then something is broken and in need of repair. Only God can deliver the satisfaction our souls desire. We will never experience true fulfillment unless we stop and sit at His feet and take in His Word. "For what does it profit a man to gain the whole world, and forfeit his soul?" (Mark 8:36 NASB).

Payoff #2: Connection.

Sometimes we create insane schedules (i.e., chronic busyness) so we can connect with others who will affirm and approve of us. Others of us engage in a more sedentary form of connectedness. Devoting an unhealthy amount of time to technology and social media, we expend massive mental energy and waste precious time maintaining virtual connections, acquiring "likes," "friends," and "followers," which gives a false sense of connection and belonging. Like the proverbial rat that learns to press a lever to receive a pellet of food, we learn to craft our posts and pictures in hopes of being rewarded by comments and traffic to our sites.

The biggest irony of pursuing these kinds of connections is that it robs us of the one connection that matters most: our relationship with God. In fact, God wired our hearts for connection, but His intent was that our need for relationships would drive us to seek a relationship with Him first. However, spending time with God requires silence and solitude that can be achieved only by disconnecting from the noise of the world and the people we are seeking to please.

Why does the thought of disconnecting make us *so* nervous? Are we afraid of what we might find in the silence and solitude? We might be scared if we've created an image of God that is contrary to His character.

Do you see God as an angry taskmaster, waiting for you to be still so He can hit you with condemnation and a list of ways to get your life together? Maybe you see a God who is disgusted by your lack of progress, and you think to spend time in His presence means experiencing His displeasure. Or perhaps you're disappointed in God because you didn't feel His presence during a time of adversity, and you've been avoiding Him ever since.

None of us wants to connect with someone whom we perceive to be angry, annoyed, or absent—even if He is sitting on a throne. Likely, all of us need the reminder from Scripture of what God is *really* like—the very One who flung the universe into place and yet cares enough to know the number of hairs on our heads (Luke 12:7).

Payoff #3: Identity.

Oftentimes our busyness stems from a desperate search for identity and purpose. Similar to throwing endless darts at the wall to see if any hit the target, we fill our calendars with dozens upon dozens of pursuits to see if we might walk away having discovered our lifelong purpose. No doubt many of us find our gifts and passions by experimentation and a process of elimination, but our identity and purpose have already been established. In fact, we find our identity and purpose only by *resting* in God rather than *serving* Him. Our identity comes from being created in the image of God (Gen. 1:26–27). Our worth should be based on who we *are* (God's beloved), not what we *do* (serve Him). Rather than follow the crowd and conform to the world's formula for finding identity and purpose, God calls us to renew our minds and find our worth in Him (Rom. 12:2). We cannot be transformed by the renewing of our minds unless we are willing to be still and meditate on His truths.

Unless we take a deeper look at the source of our chronic busyness and get honest with ourselves about the underlying motives, we will be treating only the symptoms instead of the disease. We might make minor tweaks and adjustments here and there to reduce our loads, but until we address the root of the problem, our efforts will provide only short-term solutions.

When we say yes to too many other things, we are actually saying no to God. Only God can bring the rest and satisfaction our souls crave.

Just Stop

What would God say about the problem of busyness? He might point us to Psalm 46 and His counsel to "be still, and know that I am God" (v. 10). God doesn't compete with the clamor and white noise of our busy lives. He beckons us to come before Him in silence. He wants our full, undivided attention. He wants us to cultivate space in our days to lay ourselves at His feet and breathe. He calls us to be still, or as another translation (NASB) says, "Cease striving." God calls us to cease striving to define our worth by our accomplishments. Cease striving to gain the approval of others. Cease striving to be important in the eyes of the world. Cease striving to lay up riches. Cease striving to find satisfaction in things that won't deliver on what they promise. Cease striving to give our time to people, events, and causes that won't matter a year from now. Cease striving to win God's love with acts of service. Cease striving to escape through busyness. Cease striving and know He is God—and we're not.

The original Hebrew word for "striving" or "still" is *râphâh* (raw-faw'), meaning to "slacken," much like a rope or strap that is pulled too tight and needs to be loosened.[1] It reminds me of a recent wrestling match I had with my grandson's car seat in my vehicle's backseat. He was old enough to face forward, and for months, when I snapped the straps into the base of the seat, the straps that overlapped his chest fit snugly. But then he had a sudden growth spurt. One afternoon, when I went to buckle him into his seat, the straps that overlapped his chest were suddenly too tight. I pulled and tugged with great effort until I was finally able to click the straps into the base. However, my grandson would have none of it. He immediately objected with, "No! Too tight, Mimi! Owie, owie!" Immediately I unbuckled the straps and spent the next two hours trying to find the magic mechanism that would release and slacken them. (Trust me; an engineering degree is required to figure out today's car seats. I nearly lost my religion in the process.)

Many of us refuse to make adjustments and slacken the hold busyness has on our lives. We're gasping for breath and longing for relief, all the while in control of the mechanism that would loosen the straps and release us to rest. When we deny our bodies necessary rest, we increase our risk of stress-related illnesses. From a spiritual perspective, a lack of rest can make us more vulnerable to temptations of every sort. We don't think clearly when our minds and bodies are forced to operate in constant overdrive. Why, then, do we take such pride in our busyness?

God would never endorse a pace that allows little time to rest and be still in His presence. Nor would He endorse a pace that leaves no margin for leisure. In fact, God modeled the need for rest in His creative order. Genesis 2:2–3 says, "And on the seventh day God finished his work that he had done, and he rested on the seventh day from all his work that he had done. So God blessed the seventh day and made it holy, because on it God rested from all his work that he had done in creation."

The Hebrew word for "rest" is *shâbath*, which means "to repose," "desist from exertion," or to "cease."[2] For many of us, the Sabbath has come to represent our Sunday-morning drill of church activities. While it is technically a day that has been set apart for rest, Sunday can be as exhausting as any other day of the week.

The purpose of the Sabbath is to catch our breath and reflect on what God has done, both in the beauty of His creation and in His redemptive work in our lives through Christ. He also gave us the Sabbath as a day to slacken the grip of busyness and remember to breathe.

Slow and Steady Wins the Race

"Mimi, I get out and smell the fowders."

I was pushing my two-year-old grandson in his stroller on a

walk one afternoon when he spotted a patch of yellow wildflowers. Actually, they were weeds, but I wasn't about to dampen his enthusiasm and wide-eyed wonder. I stopped the stroller and lifted him out so he could engage in his ritual of picking flowers for every relative on the family tree. One at a time he picked each flower, smelled it, announced the fortunate recipient, and toddled back to the stroller to lay it gently in the basket underneath. Back and forth he went with no sense of time. As I watched him, I wondered how many moments like this I had missed with my own children, simply because I was in a hurry. Too often I had expected them to match my pace rather than slowing down to accommodate theirs. It is one of my greatest regrets. If I could have a do-over, I would commit to *less* so I could slow down and enjoy *more*. More moments rocking my babies. More moments spent standing over their cribs or beds and watching them sleep. More time to answer their bazillion curious questions. More little baby steps from the car to the house. More focused attention on what they were saying (without finishing their sentences). I've yet to meet empty nesters who regret not being *busier* in those years or wish they had sped through those years a bit faster. Not one.

In his book *The Life You've Always Wanted*, author John Ortberg said, "Hurry is not just a disordered schedule. Hurry is a disordered heart."[3] I can't help but wonder how many priceless moments and experiences we miss each day in our rush to tend to insignificant trifles of life.

Pay attention to the target of your busyness, and you will likely find the primary affection of your heart.

Is it hard for you to rest and enjoy leisure activities
because your mind remains in constant overdrive?

Do you rush around throughout your day even when it's
not necessary?

Can you "clock out" and enjoy the moment, or do you
feel anxious to get back to your frenzied pace?

If your child moves slowly, is it hard for you to be patient
with him or her?

If a conversation lingers with a friend, do you feel
an urgency to wrap it up so you can get back to
something "more productive"?

If your phone vibrates, alerting you to another incoming
text, do you feel a compulsion to check it?

Do you check your smartphone for incoming e-mail,
even though your phone will indicate when e-mail
arrives?

Is it hard for you to separate your work life from your
personal life and draw appropriate boundaries?

If you can picture yourself in these scenarios, you may need to
take a closer look at *why* you can't seem to slow down. For most, it
boils down to not having enough margin scheduled into the day. In
his book *Margin*, author Richard Swenson defined margin as "the
space between our load and our limits." He went on to say, "It is
something held in reserve for contingencies or unanticipated situations. Margin is the gap between rest and exhaustion, the space
between breathing freely and suffocating."[4]

Life has a funny way of interrupting our best-laid plans. If we
don't allow enough margin in our lives to make space for the unexpected, or even to enjoy the expected, soon we will find ourselves
rushing through life without enjoying any of it. Many of us falsely
equate motion with productivity. Ironically, the most productive

thing we can do is slow down and be present in the moment—every moment.

When I think about the difficulty of slowing down, I'm reminded of the story of Hezekiah, the king of Judah. His reign is remembered mostly for his devotion to restoring the worship of the one true God, Jehovah. However, Hezekiah is also remembered for the humility he displayed after recovering from an illness—an illness in which God intervened and extended his life by fifteen years. In response to God's divine intervention, he responded with this praise:

> What shall I say? For he has spoken to me,
>   and he himself has done it.
> I walk slowly all my years
>   because of the bitterness of my soul. (Isa. 38:15)

It took a death sentence to get Hezekiah to understand the importance of savoring the days he was given. No doubt he was forced to slow down in his illness, but he made a conscious decision to continue to "walk slowly" in the days that followed. Some people might conclude that if they had a mere fifteen years remaining, it would be necessary to hurry all the more. Not Hezekiah. Illnesses and unexpected tragedies have a way of putting priorities in perspective and reminding us that life is a gift to be savored and enjoyed. I doubt anyone lies on her deathbed and laments that she didn't work more hours (which are now fleeting), accumulate more stuff (which will turn to dust), live in a bigger house (while failing to make her current house a home), spend more time on social networking sites "liking" acquaintances' pictures (while family members and real friends sit by her bedside), or watch more reality-TV shows (while missing a thousand beautiful sunsets).

A palliative care nurse who works with patients at the end of their lives recorded their most common regrets and compiled them in a book titled *The Top Five Regrets of the Dying.* She said, "All of the men I nursed deeply regretted spending so much of their lives on the treadmill of a work existence."[5] (Due to the fact that most of her patients were from an older generation, many of the female patients had not been breadwinners.) In short, these men all wished they had slowed down and enjoyed the things that matter most.

I don't know about you, but I don't want to face my final days wishing I had lived life more unhurried, loved more in person, watched more thunderstorms roll in, chased more fireflies with my grandchildren, and unplugged more so I could tune in to the things that matter most. I want to live unhurried and savor the moments I've been given—beginning today.

Perhaps the greatest cure for our disordered hearts is to give up this silly (and exhausting) notion that breakneck busyness is the key to living life to the fullest, and instead slow down and enjoy more fully the moments that matter.

Repenting of Busyness

Busyness is not a badge of honor. It is the cry of a burned-out soul that desperately needs relief and rest. Rather than reel off a long to-do list when someone asks us if we're busy, what if we instead offer the truth?

Life is pretty crazy right now, but the truth is I made it that way. I have this weird relationship with chronic busyness, and as a result, I wear myself out trying to maintain the image that I'm wanted, needed, and valued. I feel as if I'm operating on fumes most days. I want to slow down, but I fear I might become obsolete if I do. Busyness offers me a false sense of security that an overbooked calendar implies a full and meaningful life. I'm desperate for permission to stop striving, doing, aiming, and achieving. I need someone to remind me that even when I'm still, I will matter to those who love me most and, most importantly, to God.

Isn't that what's really going on beneath the surface of our overbooked calendars?

When we brag about our crazy, busy lives on a regular basis, we reveal that something is broken deep within our souls. A chronically overbooked calendar indicates imbalance, not importance. We must admit that we do, in fact, have a choice when it comes to busyness. We are the masters over our time, not the other way around. Busyness didn't choose us. We chose it. In his book *Crazy Busy*, author Kevin DeYoung wrote, "One reason we never tame the busyness beast is because we are unwilling to kill anything. We rearrange our schedule and tighten up our breaks, but nothing improves because we haven't pruned anything."[6] We will not see lasting change until we admit that our chronic busyness is not the result of a scheduling problem, but rather a sin problem. Only a posture of sincere repentance will produce lasting change.

If you're waiting for chronic busyness to magically disappear from your calendar, you will be sorely disappointed. The old quick-fix solutions will work—for a short time—but chances are you'll gravitate right back to your same frenzied pace. Unless you decide your chronic busyness is a sin problem rather than a scheduling problem, you will continue to feel burned out, used up, half alive.

Lasting change will require a new way of thinking and a new approach to living. Only you can decide whether you're ready for such a radical change. You can keep going at the same pace, or you can decide to repent—and rest.

REST STOP April 2017

1. On a scale of 1 to 10, how comfortable are you with your current pace of life? (With 1 being "I'm not even sure I have time to answer this question" and 10 being "I am completely satisfied with the pace of my life and wouldn't change a thing.")

   About a 6, mostly happy and some times feeling over whelmed.

2. Look back over your answers to the quiz on page 7, "You might be too busy if . . ." Would you say your busyness problem is more seasonal or chronic in nature? Explain.

   Chronic. ish... I feel like I get so overwhelmed that I give up.

3. What contributes most to your feeling of overload: work, family life, or a combination of both?

   Both

4. Look back over the busyness payoffs on pages 8–12. Which payoffs lure you into the busyness trap most often?

Satisfaction + Identity

5. Is it easy for you to slow down, or do you tend to rush through your day and miss the moments that matter most? What steps might you need to take to slow down?

When I am alone its easy to slow down. Even in the cleaning, work and the to-do list. It feels like when other people are around I need to constently be doing things, acomplishing something. It tend to be more enjoyeble to do things when no one else is around because I can take my time or a break when I need to. I can not be so worried about what others think and be a joyful doer of things.

THE INTERVENTION

1. How has your soul been impacted by chronic
   busyness? Take a few minutes to think about specific
   ways busyness has taken a toll on your soul and
   impacted your relationship with the Lord. Describe
   them here:

2. If chronic busyness is a problem for you, remember
   that lasting change begins with sincere repentance.
   Acts 3:19–20 says, "Repent therefore, and turn
   back, that your sins may be blotted out, that times of
   refreshing may come from the presence of the Lord."
      The Greek word for "repent" is *mĕtanŏĕō*, and it
   means "to think differently" or "reconsider."[7] If you
   sense that God is calling you to repentance, and you
   sincerely desire to change, spend some time in prayer
   and express godly sorrow over the ways busyness has
   impacted your life and your soul. If you want to
   "think differently" when it comes to busyness, express
   your desire to God and ask Him to help you.

Describe what "thinking differently" might look like.

3. Determine what action steps you will take to demonstrate your declaration of repentance (be as specific as possible). Examples:

I will resign xx position (if God so leads, of course).

I will not accept any more volunteer positions until I gain better control of the problem.

I will limit the number of after-school-related activities for my children in order to gain more margin.

I will not say yes unless I have first talked it over with an accountability partner or my spouse.

4. Share with a trusted friend (or your group) your new insights, as well as the action steps you plan to take to help alleviate the problem of chronic busyness.

2

The Exhausting Pursuit
of Happiness

Life, liberty, and the pursuit of happiness. When our Founding Fathers dipped their quill pens in inkwells in 1776 to draft the Declaration of Independence, they declared these unalienable rights as our legacy, endowed to us by our Creator. In doing so, they sounded the gun at the start line of a rat race that would span the generations for centuries to come. The early patriarchs of our country made an assumption, and no one questioned it: personal happiness is the highest reward this earthly life can offer. However, if we examine the phrase more carefully, we'll see that the assumption operates on a faulty model. Happiness is elusive and nothing more than a temporary, fleeting emotion. Even if captured for a moment, happiness cannot deliver on its promises. To pursue happiness is akin to grasping at the wind, hoping each fistful we seize will bring the lasting satisfaction we crave in our aching souls. We can exhaust all of our time, energy, and money in its pursuits, only to be left thinking there's *got* to be more. Any time we attempt to fill our souls with temporary fillers to satisfy a permanent longing, the result will always be unrest.

I recently stumbled across this nugget of vintage wisdom while reading an article in an 1894 edition of *Ladies' Home Journal*:

> In this busy rush of life, we all need to pause now and then to take a breath. We are too busy planning for happiness in the future to enjoy life in the present. As Sydney Smith says, "We are, in our search for happiness, like an absent-minded man looking for his hat, while all the time it is on his head." We are so busy getting ready to live, that life is over before we have time to realize what we have.[1]

The writer of the article beautifully summed up the futility of the pursuit of happiness: "We are too busy planning for happiness in the future to enjoy life in the present."[2]

On one hand, I can take comfort in knowing this "busy rush of life" is not exclusive to our present times. A reference to the 1890s might conjure up a picture of "simpler" times when women sat in quilting circles and caught up on the latest town gossip (childcare not included); however, life then was anything but simple. People were busy, but most of their busyness was rooted in sheer survival. They certainly weren't posting their handmade quilts to Pinterest boards or folding them neatly at the end of the bed as an accent to their Egyptian cotton duvets. If women then could see a glimpse of the modern-day devices and amenities of today, I imagine they'd be scratching their heads in confusion over why we feel the same busy rush of life. Any time we have gained with our time-saving devices has been filled with more busyness. How did we get here?

For many, busyness is rooted in the ever-exhausting pursuit of happiness. It looms before us like a dangling carrot, promising to satisfy our souls in a thousand different ways. A thinner body, another child, an advanced degree, a promotion, a larger bank account, a more attentive husband. Try as we may, happiness is nothing more than an overnight guest, refusing to take up permanent residence in our hearts. It's ironic; isn't it? We exhaust ourselves in pursuing that which we think will bring us happiness only to discover that our souls lie wasted and pale, worn and lifeless. The pursuit of happiness only burdens our souls with more unrest. If we want to give our souls a rest, we must learn to "pause now and then to take breath," as the 1894 article recommends. In that pause, we just might discover that the happiness we yearn for is right at our fingertips.

The If-Then Trap

You can learn a lot about people's personal pursuits of happiness by what they post on their refrigerators. Take, for example, a woman who visited my church many years ago. She and her husband were new to Austin and had just had their first child. I signed up to take a meal to their home, and when I arrived to drop it off, the mom was nursing the baby. I offered to put the meal away in the refrigerator, and she gladly accepted the extra help. When I went to open her refrigerator, I couldn't help but notice that she had tacked a couple of interesting pictures to the door (a pre-Pinterest pinboard).

One picture featured a very slim model in a swimsuit, perfectly toned without a hint of cellulite (or body fat, for that matter)—a picture obviously pulled from a fashion magazine. The model's body shape matched about .001 percent of the female population, thanks to a steady diet of lettuce leaves and rice cakes. The other picture tacked to her refrigerator door featured an advertisement promoting a new subdivision being built in Austin. Curious, I yelled into the living room, "Hey, what's up with the pictures on your refrigerator? Are you guys about to move?"

She replied, "I wish! I put those on my fridge as motivation— you know, to remind me of my goals and where I'm headed in life. I won't be happy until I drop this extra weight and move out of this rental neighborhood."

She held a brand-new baby in her arms and sat in a nice living room with a roof overhead, but she thought she had to have a better body and different house to be happy. She was caught up in the if-then trap. Her happiness was held hostage by an uncertain outcome or set of conditions.

If _____, then I will be happy.

When it comes to the pursuit of happiness, what is on your if-then list? Try these on for size:

- If I could find a good guy and settle down, then I'd be happier.
- If I could lose ten pounds, then I'd be happier.
- If my husband would start going to church with me, then I'd be happier.
- If I had a marriage like _____, then I'd be happier.
- If my marriage hadn't ended in divorce, then I'd be happier.

- If I lived in a better neighborhood, then I'd be happier.
- If I didn't have to work and could stay home with my kids, then I'd be happier.
- If I could get out of this house and go back to work, then I'd be happier.
- If I didn't have to work so many long hours, then I'd be happier.
- If my kids were as well-behaved as _____, then I'd be happier.
- If I hadn't had such a rough childhood, then I'd be happier.

Hear me out. Striving to improve our circumstances does not constitute misplaced priorities or misdirected energies. The problem comes when we postpone our happiness for *someday* and, in doing so, miss the blessing that is *today*. Psalm 118:24 reminds us, "This is the day the LORD has made; let us rejoice and be glad in it" (HCSB). Searching the Bible for references to *happiness* or *happy*, we discover roughly about thirty (depending on the translation). On the other hand, the words *joy* and *rejoice* appear more than three hundred times.[3] Our culture may be focused on the pursuit of happiness, but God cares far more about our pursuits of joy.

The Hebrew word for "rejoice" is *gûwl*, and it means "to spin round; be glad, be joyful."[4] When was the last time you remember spinning around in a fit of joy? When I read that definition, the first image that came to my mind was an old home movie filmed when I was a little girl. I was about four years old, and it was Christmas morning. I was spinning around and around with a candy cane in my mouth and my arms opened wide. In the backdrop was my newly acquired Christmas morning loot—a wooden refrigerator with a matching oven and sink—sitting next to the Christmas tree. Santa had gotten my letter, and I was a happy, happy girl.

Why is the spinning around type of rejoicing typically reserved for children? Or Christmas morning? Why do we see joy expressed only on a cheesy episode of *The Bachelor*, when the bachelorette contestant runs into the bachelor's waiting arms and he lifts her up and spins her around, happy to see her after a brief separation? Of course, this type of rejoicing is a cheap knock-off to true joy. It is more like a temporary burst of euphoria. The "spin round" type of joy spoken of in Psalm 118 occurs daily, stemming from an unwavering sense of gratitude.

In one of my vintage copies of *Ladies' Home Journal* from 1896, a popular author of a featured column for young girls shared, "I know of a woman who used to say she could not ask God to bless her—she always asked Him to open her eyes to see her blessings."[5] Attitude truly is everything. Blessings surround us, but we cannot see them because sight is limited to elusive if-then expectations. Joy requires panoramic vision rather than tunnel vision. Experiencing joy requires us to shift our focus from what we want *someday* to what we already have *today*.

Every day is a gift from God. We are alive. We are breathing. When we wake up in the morning, approximately 960 waking minutes are available to us that day to enjoy and savor. Or not. Even if the day doesn't go so well, chances are we'll be granted another 960 minutes to give it another go tomorrow. When we attach our happiness to a list of if-then conditions, we miss the joy found in the 960 moments God has already given us today. Once gone, we can never get them back.

If we want to experience more than what a temporary state of happiness can provide, we must make joy our aim. True joy is not the result of an outcome but is, rather, an attitude. What if every morning we decided to get out of bed and boldly declare, "This is the day the Lord has made. I will rejoice and be glad in it"?

Bonus points if you can spin around while proclaiming it. Extra bonus points if you can say it with conviction before your first cup of coffee.

Overexpectations

While scrolling recently through my newsfeed on Facebook, I came across a series of pictures posted by a mother who had just thrown a first birthday party for her only child. The parents had spared no expense. The bash featured many elements you might find at a wedding reception: a professional photographer and videographer, a catered meal, a photo booth. Each little guest received personalized sippy-cup party favors. The birthday girl even had two wardrobe changes to accommodate for the messiness after she was coaxed (as per the script) to dig into her own personal "smash cake." (In my day, we solved this problem with something called a bib.) Her pre-cake outfit was a darling tutu ensemble with a matching head-band, and the skirted high chair tray coordinated with her outfit perfectly. Yes, the high chair matched her outfit.

But before I could cast judgment on this excessive party-planning mom, God nudged my heart with a reminder of a parti-cular birthday party I had organized for my oldest child when he turned five. Even by pre-Pinterest birthday-party standards, the party was a bit over the top. Okay, a lot. His pirate-themed party was the talk of the preschool. The invitations were professionally printed on pirate-themed cardstock with the following poem I had crafted for the occasion:

Ahoy Mates, strong and bold,
Ryan Courtney is five years old!
Come be a pirate for a spell
And to his island, we'll all set sail
For a morning filled with fun and pleasure,
Lots of goodies and buried treasure.
He's asking his friends not to fear,
But Captain Hook may even appear!
So don't miss out on this fun-filled day,
And the game of pirates we will play!

But wait, there's more. Accompanying the invitation was a treasure map designed, yes, by yours truly.

TREASURE MAP

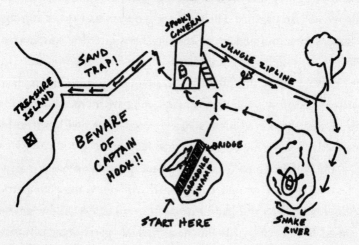

It was printed on parchment paper, and I even took care to burn the edges of each one to give the maps an old, weathered look. One of my friends whose son was invited claimed that her boy studied the map for hours after receiving it in the mail, intent on decoding the exact location of the buried treasure.

On the day of the party, each child had an opportunity to complete the obstacle course printed on the treasure map. The course included a plank-walk over a kiddie pool filled with plastic alligators, a trip through our playhouse that had been temporarily converted to a makeshift "spooky cavern," and a zip-line across the lawn that eventually led to the play area where buried treasure could be found under designated Xs spray-painted on pea gravel. Assuming, of course, the children could evade the notorious Captain Hook and his relentless attempts to interrupt their brave adventure. (My husband is still angry with me to this day for making him dress up in the rented costume, complete with a black wig, red coat with gold-braided trim, and white ruffled jabot.) Never mind that some of the children, who are now adults, are probably still having night terrors as a result of being chased around the backyard by my husband waving his plastic hook hand at them. Hopefully, the pirate's booty helped make up for any trauma they experienced.

Two decades later we still laugh about the over-the-top pirate party. The funniest memory (maybe not so much at the time) was when I realized (about an hour into the party) that the birthday boy was missing. I found him inside the house playing with a new LEGO set in a corner of the living room. When I asked him what he was doing and reminded him of the pirate bash being held in his honor in the backyard, he told me very matter-of-factly that he was ready for his friends to go home so he could play with his new toys. This might explain why my third (and last) child's five-year birthday amounted to a dozen donuts, a helium balloon, and a round of "Happy Birthday" sung by his family members around the kitchen table. You live and learn.

If I were completely honest about my overzealous party-planning episode, I would admit that the party merely manifested a much deeper issue. I *desperately* wanted to be a good mother. And good mothers provide perfect, happily-ever-after memories for their children, right? If only my son could remember the memory! Oh, the irony. I wonder how much of our striving is rooted in a subconscious attempt to maintain a happily-forever-after-all-the-time façade.

Maybe you can relate to the tug-of-war. Why aim for *adequate* when you can take it up a notch and aim for *exceptional*? *Adequate* seems so inadequate when you log onto your favorite social media sites and see the highlight reels of everyone else's *exceptional* lives. The Pinterest-perfect parties with paper straws in mason jars and string lights hanging from the trees. *Exceptional.* The braggadocio about kids making the honor roll, the A-team, or the homecoming court. *Exceptional.* The kitchen remodels with white marble countertops, double ovens, and stainless steel Sub-Zero refrigerators (whatever those are). *Exceptional.* The steady stream of creatively inspired family photos taken on white-sand beaches or in front of rustic barns. *Exceptional.* The status updates of what friends are serving for dinner. *Exceptional.* Bonus points if it involves fresh herbs picked from the backyard garden. *Beyond exceptional.* Or that mom who juggles as much as you do and *still* has time to train for a marathon. *Exceptional.* And she's a tiny size four to boot. *Disgustingly exceptional.* (And possible grounds for unfriending.)

Add to this drive for excellence the constant bombardment from ads that taunt us with the message that slim, pretty, charming, sexy, trendy, and fashionable are guaranteed pathways to happy, exceptional lives. The wrinkle creams and fad diets. The lash-extending mascara. The hundred-calorie yogurt that promises to make us bikini-ready by summer. Not to mention those darn targeted ads that assault us on Facebook and land in our inbox uninvited. How did they know I have a muffin top that needs "melting" or a master bath that needs remodeling? Leave me alone, and let me enjoy my post-fifty, but *adequate*, midsection; my short and stubby, but *adequate*, eyelashes; and my outdated, but *adequate*, master bath.

Jesus had some dear friends, Mary and Martha. He paid them a visit on His travels, and Martha—like a lot of us probably would—kicked into gear, cooking the perfect meal for her guest. Mary, however, sat at Jesus' feet, listening to Him speak and soaking in His presence (Luke 10:38–42 NKJV). When Jesus reprimanded Martha for "much serving" and commended her sister, Mary, for choosing the "one thing . . . needed," He was not condemning service but rather making a statement about *much* serving. The Greek word for "much" is *pŏlus*, which means "largely" or "abundant."[6] One Bible commentary says, "Some expositors have taken the expression to mean 'a single dish is sufficient' for my entertainment."[7] Another commentary notes, "Whereas Martha was in care to provide *many* dishes of meat, there was occasion but for one, one would be enough."[8] Martha's striving to provide an exceptional meal caused her to miss a truly exceptional experience.

What if you took your expectations down a notch and gave yourself permission to let go of *exceptional* and make peace with *adequate*? If you are weary from chasing after a self-imposed standard that is impossible to reach, take a lesson from Martha and set your soul free. One dish is enough. Just one.

Those Darn Joneses

"Your neighbors will be jealous." It's a simple slogan on a billboard advertising a new housing subdivision on a road I travel frequently. Love it or hate it, the slogan unapologetically taps into our unexpressed, unacknowledged desire to impress others. In the book *The Overspent American*, author Juliet Schor suggests this keep-up-with-the-Joneses mentality has been around for quite some time.

Seventeenth- and eighteenth-century Italian nobles built opulent palaces with beautiful façades and, within those façades, placed tiles engraved with the words *Pro Invidia* ("to be envied"). At the turn of the century, the wealthy published the menus of their dinner parties in the newspapers. And fifty years ago, American social climbers bought fake "ancestor portraits" to hang in their libraries.[9]

Today the desire to impress has shifted from putting menus in newspapers to posting on Facebook and Instagram.

In Ecclesiastes 4:4, King Solomon, in his own quest to discover the meaning of life, concluded, "And I saw that all toil and all achievement spring from one person's envy of another. This too is meaningless, a chasing after the wind" (NIV). When I was studying economics in college (my major), I became well-acquainted with the concept of *conspicuous consumption*. If you're not familiar with the term, it amounts to "buying unnecessary and expensive products and services as a way to show off wealth."[10] The term was coined by US economist Thorstein Veblen, who wrote extensively on the topic more than a century ago.

In his classic work *The Theory of the Leisure Class*, Veblen suggested that "the members of each stratum accept as their ideal of decency the scheme of life in vogue in the next higher stratum, and bend their energies to live up to that ideal."[11] In other words, each social status has its ideal "perfect life" of a higher social status and strives to live up to that ideal. Sound familiar? The habit of comparing our social status with that of our neighbors, Facebook friends, or others' picture-perfect Pinterest pinboards seems to be ingrained within us.

Fifty years ago our neighbors were just that: our immediate neighbors. If the mom down the street got a new station wagon with wood paneling on the sides, just about every housewife on the block would be guilty of making a mental comparison and finding herself lacking. Pretty soon thereafter more station wagons would begin to pop up in the neighborhood. In fact, our economy is built on the premise that we will compare our social status to that of others a notch (or more) above us and, as Veblen predicted, "bend our energies to live up to that ideal." Unfortunately our comparisons today are no longer limited to what our geographical neighbors have. Thanks (or no thanks) to technology, we are exposed to just about every social status and lifestyle imaginable and are readily encouraged to consume well beyond our means—even if it results in financial ruin.

In our culture we aren't used to having to wait for things. In fact, the system of credit card financing is built on the backs of consumers who can't wait and are willing to borrow against tomorrow to have what they want today. Why wait for "better" when we can have better right now for a so-called "small, minimum monthly payment"? It's no wonder the majority of people in our country are in debt up to their eyeballs, with little to nothing set aside for emergencies, much less the future.

While I was once again thumbing through one of my vintage copies of *Ladies' Home Journal* (this one from 1894), I stumbled upon a fascinating article titled "When There Is a Surplus." The author offered this advice:

> Perhaps there is no happier time in the housewife's life than the day in which she begins to realize that the hardest part of her home-making is passed. After struggles and self-denials business prosperity makes it possible for her to indulge her individual taste and fancies. Now the question confronts her, "What shall be done with the surplus which remains after the legitimate needs of housekeeping have been satisfied?"[12]

She went on to advise the following:

> It is better to have a large income and a small house than to reverse the conditions. The first point then, is to remain in the small home until there is a good working surplus, instead of moving into larger quarters with no margin for increased expenses. Granted, however, that the housewife does stay in the old, plain home until, without anxiety or debt, she can move to a handsome house on a more fashionable street, and there yet remains a surplus. What shall she do with it?[13]

The author goes on to suggest that "the surplus" can be used to purchase a bigger home or add luxury accoutrements such as silver, crystal, rugs, art, and books. Long before home mortgages and credit cards, people learned to live within their means because they had no other option. The reward came later when they had set aside enough money to enjoy the finer things. Today's society has completely reversed that concept. Most of us will overbuy on a home, charge the majority of the possessions that fill it, and spend years trying to undo the damage. Most of us will give it little thought because the norm is to "have it and have it now." Until the bills come due, of course, and the buzz quickly wears off. The real price is not only the debt but the peace of mind forfeited in the process.

According to research released by the American Psychological Association, money, work, and the economy are the biggest causes of Americans' stress.[14] Our culture of upscale spending is taking a toll on our souls. Proverbs 22:7 reminds us that "the borrower is the slave of the lender." I am not suggesting that it is evil to take out a mortgage on a home, but I do think it's important to "own our lifestyle" (literally, without debt) as much as possible. One simple discipline my husband cultivated early in our marriage was a commitment not to finance anything unless it could be paid in full at the end of each month. The only exceptions were our home and cars. We made sure that our mortgage was well under the range for which we qualified so we didn't fall into the trap of being "house poor" (with little to no margin left over to enjoy life). We also bought used cars so we didn't owe a large amount of money on our vehicles. In the early years I harassed my husband about his frugality, especially when I fell into the trap of comparing myself to others. Twenty-eight years later I am grateful for his frugality and refusal to live beyond our means.

In 1 John 2, the apostle John warned of the dangers of comparing ourselves to others and chasing after worldly desires:

Do not love the world or the things in the world. If anyone loves the world, the love of the Father is not in him. For all that is in the world—the desires of the flesh and the desires of the eyes and pride of life [or, the pride in possessions]—is not from the Father but is from the world. And the world is passing away along with its desires, but whoever does the will of God abides forever. (vv. 15–17)

The Greek word for "eyes" in the passage above is *ophthalmos*, from which we derive our English word *ophthalmology*. The word is defined in the Greek as "vision or envy from the jealous side-glance."[15] The passage does not denounce worldly things. Rather, it warns against putting too much emphasis on things that have no eternal or lasting value.

Henry David Thoreau is quoted as having said, "The cost of a thing is the amount of what I will call life which is required to be exchanged for it, immediately or in the long run."[16] This is true of our possessions whether financed or paid off. Our souls crave simplicity. If we want to experience true rest in our souls, we must be willing to examine our attitudes about money and, more importantly, the role we believe money plays when it comes to the pursuit of happiness.

The Good Life

"Ah, the good life." Chances are you've mumbled the phrase before, possibly while sipping on a fruity drink under a beach umbrella with a book in your lap and the expanse of the ocean before you. Or perhaps you've said a variation of it in a slightly sarcastic yet wistful tone after catching a glimpse of someone else's "good life." You know, the one who posted a picture of her boarding pass to Cabo. After the picture of her enjoying lunch with a fun group of friends the week before. Which may have followed the picture she posted of the roses her husband sent her for no reason at all. (To which I say, "One, two, three strikes, and you're out! Time to hide you from my newsfeed.")

Each one of us has a picture of what constitutes "the good life," whether or not we've consciously given it much thought. We tune in to TV shows such as *Mega Mansions* and see the marble floors in the grand foyers, double winding staircases, and master bedroom closets that are the size of most of our bedrooms and conclude that money does, in fact, buy happiness. However, if the cameras offered a sneak peek into the closet of the souls of the mega-wealthy, we might be surprised to find that the rich and famous are not any happier than the housekeeping staffs that clean their homes. In fact, they just might be miserable.

Take it from someone who should know. Austrian business-man Karl Rabeder lived the lifestyle of the mega-rich—luxury cars, private planes, a villa in the Alps, and a farmhouse in Provence. He experienced the kind of lifestyle many of us could only dream about, yet he concluded it wasn't the life for him. His life-changing epiphany came while on a long, three-week vacation in Hawaii; he claims he "realized how horrible, soulless and without feeling the five star lifestyle is."[17]

His net worth hovered around $4.5 million, but he decided to liquidate it all after his life-changing realization and used the money to fund charities in Latin America.

Ironically, many of the perks commonly associated with the "good life" can lead to a greater misery and emptiness than had they not been attained at all. And therein lies the trap. The good life we tend to imagine is always an upgraded version of our current life. Even if we reach the pinnacle of what we define as "the good life," "better" will always lie just beyond our reach.

Many of the world's greatest philosophers have pondered this idea of "the good life." In fact, Aristotle unpacked the question: "What is the good life for man?" His answer was simple: a life of happiness. He rejected the common definition of happiness as a subjective state of mind and viewed it instead as an end goal achieved by reflecting on the totality of one's life. In other words, he believed a life could not be deemed as "happy" until the end.[18] In essence, the good life is experienced over time.

What if I told you Jesus has offered us a better option to the good life about which so many of us have dreamed? A life that we cannot purchase but that will bring rest to our aching souls.

The Abundant Life

"Wouldn't God want me to be happy?" This was the last thing one of my friends said to me before she cut off all communication and basically ended the friendship. She had decided to leave her husband for another man she had met just months prior. Her husband was blindsided when she told him she wanted to end the marriage, and he begged her to stay. He offered to do whatever was necessary to mend their marriage, but to no avail. They had two young children, and she had even talked about having another child the last time I saw her, which made her announcement all the more surreal. At her husband's request, I made one last appeal and asked her to give her marriage a chance, but it fell on deaf ears. She had already made up her mind. She claimed this other man loved her in a way her husband could not. "He makes me happy. Wouldn't God want me to be happy?"

It's been more than two decades since I last saw her, but I've thought a lot about her parting statement in the years that have passed. I don't remember exactly what I said as a response, but if I could get a do-over, I'd offer this: "Actually, God is far more concerned with our *holiness* than our *happiness*." Not that my perspective would have changed her mind. And the truth is I have no right to criticize my friend's skewed theology. I may not have traveled the same path and made the same choices, but I can think of plenty of times in my own life when I've prioritized the pursuit of happiness over the pursuit of holiness.

In John 10:10, Jesus declared, "I came that they may have life and have it abundantly." The Greek word for "abundantly" is *pĕrissŏs*, and it means "superabundant (in quantity) or superior (in quality); exceeding abundantly above."[19] While we tend to look to the world to find happiness and a superior life, Jesus was saying in essence, "I have the answer. Look to Me. Follow Me. What I'm offering is far superior to the off-brand, knock-off version of happiness the world is offering." Why, then, do we continue to engage in the chase? Interestingly, Jesus made this bold claim just after saying, "The thief comes only to steal and kill and destroy."

If you were the enemy and were hell-bent (literally, in this case) on rendering your opponent powerless and ineffective, the best strategy you could employ would be to divert believers' attention from their greatest source of power. Offer them false substitutes that promise a happier, more fulfilling life, luring them into a subtle sense of complacency. The strategy would be all the better if you could get a mass of God's followers to engage in groupthink and believe they were all on the right track, never questioning whether the never-ending pursuit of happiness was actually a lie. No wonder so many believers feel unrest in their souls.

In Colossians 3:1–2, Paul exhorted believers to "seek the things that are above, where Christ is, seated at the right hand of God. Set your minds on things that are above, not on things that are on earth." The Greek word for "seek" is *zētĕō*, and it means "to worship (God), or to plot (against life); to desire, endeavour."[20] Let that definition sink in for a minute. It beautifully describes the tug-of-war raging in our souls on a daily basis. One Bible commentary notes,

> *Things on earth* are here set in opposition to *things above.* We must not dote upon them, nor expect too much from them, that we may set our affections on heaven; for heaven and earth are contrary one to the other, and a supreme regard to both is inconsistent; and the prevalence of our affection to one will proportionately weaken and abate our affection to the other.[21]

If we want to make Christ our primary pursuit, we must resist the lie that the baubles and shiny trinkets of this world can satisfy our souls.

The Greek word for "set" is *phrŏnĕō*, which means "to exercise the mind, to interest oneself in (with concern or obedience); set the affection on."[22] Paul was not encouraging a disdain for material things. Every physical thing God created is good. Instead, Paul was warning believers against affections other than God that become the center of our worship and our lives. Is Christ our primary affection? Do we exercise our minds and set our affections on Him daily? Setting our affections on Christ is not a one-time exercise or a super-spiritual gift that magically descends on us when we pray to receive Christ. Believers must consciously and continually decide to make Him their primary pursuit and fight hard to keep Him there. One Bible commentary says, "The first (to seek) suggests striving; the second (to set) suggests concentrating."[23]

Are you worn-out from engaging in the exhausting pursuit of happiness? You will continue to experience unrest in your soul until Jesus becomes your primary pursuit. You can keep chasing the world's brand of happiness, or you can take Jesus up on His offer to supersize the deal and experience a life that is exceedingly, abundantly above anything the world has to offer. The choice is yours.

REST STOP

1. When it comes to the pursuit of happiness, what is (or has been) on your if-then list? "If _____ _____, then I will be happy." Is finding joy in the present moment difficult for you?

2. In what areas of your life do you need to aim for *adequate* rather than *exceptional*?

3. Do you struggle with "conspicuous consumption"? How has this affected your soul? Think of an example of a time when managing your possessions has caused you to miss out on life and the moments that matter most. Share the example.

4. What is your idea of the "good life"? How has this robbed you at times of the abundant life of which Jesus speaks?

5. If you were honest, what would you say has been your primary pursuit: the world's idea of happiness or Jesus' promise of the abundant life?

6. What are some steps you can take to "seek the things that are above," setting your mind "on things that are above"?

THE INTERVENTION

1. How has your soul been impacted by the pursuit of happiness? Take a few minutes to think about specific instances when chasing happiness took a toll on your soul and impacted your relationship with the Lord. List them here.

2. If the pursuit of happiness has been a problem for you, remember that lasting change begins with sincere repentance. Acts 3:19–20 says, "Repent therefore, and turn back, that your sins may be blotted out, that times of refreshing may come from the presence of the Lord."

   Recall that the Greek word for "repent" is *mĕtanŏĕō*, and it means "to think differently" or "reconsider."[24] If you feel that repentance is in order and you sincerely desire to "think differently," express that to God in prayer.

3. Describe how you now "think differently" about the pursuit of happiness.

4. Write down the steps that you need to take in order to demonstrate your repentance with action (be as specific as possible).

3

Tethered Souls

Is your heart racing? Are your palms sweating? Do you have a compulsive urge to glance incessantly at your phone? If so, you could be suffering from a fairly new condition called "Text Bubble Anxiety." No, really, it's a thing. I'm not making this up. A recent article claims the tiny, gray text bubble that houses the three-dot ellipsis (an iPhone feature) is causing an extreme level of distress among some iPhone users as they wait in anticipation for a text reply. The technical term for the stress-inducing ellipsis is the "typing awareness indicator."

So... Wanna hang out this weekend?

Delivered

For those not familiar with this feature, it notifies the texter (the person sending the text) that the textee (the one receiving the text) has not only received the text but is also in the process of drafting a reply. And to add even more anticipation to the moment, the text bubble is not static. It shows highlighting motion of one dot following another, indicating that a totally awesome reply is in the works. The anxiety stems from the fact that the original sender is held hostage by the taunting text bubble, her eyes glued to the screen until the much-anticipated reply arrives.

Therein lies the problem. A reply doesn't always arrive. Letdown ensues. Paranoia sets in. "Why did they abandon the text?" "I know she read it and started to reply. Is she having second thoughts?" "Was it something I said?" (The texter then rechecks the message sent to ensure proper verbiage and emoticon usage.) The second-guessing will be replaced by a sense of low-level rejection. A virtual snub, if you will.

You may think such connection to a cyber-reply sounds ridiculous, until you're the one waiting for the reply. Imagine being single (and some of you are). You had an amazing first date with a guy you'd love to go out with again. Based on his cues and even a verbal suggestion on his part that you "get together again," you conclude the feelings are mutual. The next day you draft a polite text thanking him for dinner and a great time together. "Hey, just wanted to say thanks again for a wonderful evening." You don't want to be too pushy, so even though you're tempted to follow up with "I'd love to get together again sometime," you opt instead for the safer option: "Hope you're having a great day!" Heart beating, palms sweating, blood pressure rising, you wait. Fortunately, you don't have to wait long; within seconds, you see the text bubble ellipsis on your screen. You let out a huge sigh of relief. And then you wait . . . and you wait . . . and you wait.

The text bubble ellipsis remains on the screen, its motion taunting you with a false hope that your message is being immediately addressed. Seconds pass, and you hope he is taking his time to craft a funny and creative response of mutual approval. Then seconds stretch into minutes and you begin to wonder, *Maybe he didn't really have a good time; maybe he doesn't want to lead me on with a reply.* After a few more agonizing minutes, if you're an optimist, you imagine him drafting a novel on the other end, which will end with a request for another date. And then you get *nothing.* Nada. Zilch. The text bubble ellipsis eventually disappears, and your heart sinks. Or maybe you did get a reply, but instead of it being the long response you thought was coming (including an invitation to another date, at least one exclamation point, and a happy face emoticon), you get a "You're welcome. Same to you."

You sigh heavily. You check and recheck your original text to better understand the context of his vague reply. You then proceed to hypothesize a dozen or more possible explanations, most of which are not in your favor. You have no choice (okay, actually you do, but more about that later). You take a screenshot of the conversation and send it to your best friend for analysis. You experience a flashback to your middle school days when you'd send your best friend on a mission to find out who your crush liked. And then you'd wait. And hope. And bite your nails. And assume the worst. And make a mental note to ask your mom later if you could transfer to a different school. The taunting ellipsis dredges up similar emotions. Who would think three tiny dots on a phone screen could have so much power?

This may sound ridiculous, but I never would have been able

to endure the text bubble ellipsis in my dating phase of life. Or its close cousin, the "message read" indicator offered on many social networking platforms. Rather than brush off this perceived snub and go back to whatever I was doing before the text or message was sent, I most likely would have lapsed into full-out pity-party mode, which, in its tamest form, would involve a box of Cheez-Its and back-to-back episodes of *Gilligan's Island*. To be honest, I've felt anxious at times over e-mailing a friend and realizing later that I never got a reply. For that reason, I can certainly understand how that wee little text bubble ellipsis can take hours off a person's life.

Gary Klassen, the principal architect at BlackBerry, said the ellipsis is "like eye contact in a conversation: You know if they're paying attention."[1] I have to wonder if these devices that were supposed to make our lives easier have, at the end of the day, made our lives far more complicated—and our souls empty and aching for relief.

Being Present

On a recent visit to my neighborhood park with my two-and-a-half-year-old grandson, I couldn't help but notice that the majority of parents were more engaged with their smartphones than with their children. One little girl in particular caught my eye. She was playing in the sand pit area where my grandson was busying himself with a dump truck. She was walking along the railroad ties that contained the sand pit while her dad held her hand to balance her. In his other hand, he held his phone and scrolled with his thumb, appearing to read an article or perhaps surf a social networking newsfeed. His daughter was quite proud of herself for not falling off the railroad ties, and every so often she would look up to see if he was watching her accomplish this miraculous (for her) feat. The dad was clueless, missing her cues for focused attention. In doing so, he sent a clear message to his daughter: whatever was on that small, four-inch screen was of far greater interest and importance than her triumphal mastery of the timber beams. Her look of disappointment said it all. He missed that too.

As I raced my grandson down a double slide (and let him win, of course), I noticed a mother sitting by herself at a picnic table, also engaged with her phone. Eventually her son joined my grandson and me in our slide race. Every now and then she glanced up and offered a vague acknowledgment to her son's chimes of, "Mama, watch this? Did you see that?" She'd say something like, "Yes, Caleb, that's awesome!" and then lock her eyes back onto her screen, looking at something of monumental importance, like a text or Facebook post or Instagram feed. Who knows what had captured her attention, but it certainly wasn't her son. I know it's impossible to offer our children uninterrupted, focused attention every waking moment of their day, and even if such attentiveness were possible, it would be overindulgent to do so. But surely we can strike a healthier balance between our actual, happening-right-now lives and the technology we use. When the two become too enmeshed, the people we love suffer the consequences.

Before I can pass judgment on anyone, I need to confess that after that trip to the park, my grandson and I went home, and he wanted to play a game of Barnyard Bingo. I got the game down from a shelf and told him to get it all set up on the living room floor and we'd play. I then proceeded to open my laptop and put on my reading glasses in a quick attempt to check my e-mail to make sure nothing urgent had landed in my inbox while I was at the park. Before I could even click over to my e-mail, my grandson said, "Mimi, take off your glasses." He had somehow made the connection that when Mimi puts on her reading glasses, she puts off her grandson. Busted. I took off my glasses, closed my laptop, and joined my grandson on the floor. Whatever was in my inbox could certainly wait another thirty minutes until he went down for a nap.

I don't watch my grandson on a full-time basis, but I can completely understand how mothers with little ones would feel the pull to social media and texting as a means to break up the day and find connection with someone who was more than two feet tall and who could engage in a two-way conversation. My generation had its own fair share of distractions, but nothing compares to the myriad diversions in today's culture. I lament about the addictive power of technology on young people today, but I have no doubts that I would have been the mother glued to her phone at the park had it been an available distraction when I was a young mom. Or perhaps I would have been the one trying to snap the perfect picture, find a flattering filter, and add a laugh-out-loud clever caption that would generate a large number of "likes" and comments and boost my fledgling self-esteem. At least for a moment. I feel the pull of technology myself as it is. I can't imagine how powerful the pull would have been had technology been available during an earlier chapter of life, when I was searching for my identity and prone to people-pleasing behaviors.

The jury is still out when it comes to the long-term effects smartphones (and other electronic devices) will have on our everyday lives. I'm certainly not advocating that we revert back to simpler times with rotary dial phones, snail mail, and television sets with four channels and a rabbit-ear antenna. As much as I complain, I don't miss the days of fold-up navigation maps (that I could never fold back up) and missed phone calls on landlines, sans call-waiting, and answering machines. (Remember those?) Besides, it's too late. We can't un-ring this bell. Or chime. Or fight song. Or whatever notification alert we've chosen among the hundreds on our smartphones. Most of our children will grow up with constant accessibility and unfettered access to information around the clock. They have known nothing else.

In addition to *Ladies' Home Journal*, I also own a small collection of vintage *Seventeen* magazines that I once used as a fun resource when I spoke to audiences of teen girls. In an edition dating back to 1949, one article, titled "Cybernetics," offered teen girls a tiny glimpse into the future of "thinking machines," as computers were dubbed. The author predicted with fair accuracy the role computers might play in the future. He described one such computer, housed in New York City, so enormous that it filled three walls and took eighteen months to build. The article speculated, with a tone of utter amazement, about a time in the distant future when these "thinking machines" could be accessed by individuals for non-mathematical purposes, such as "playing a game of checkers."[2] Little did the author know just how far the scope of this "new technology" would span into the future. Or that playing a game of checkers with a device would be considered mundane by today's standards, having been displaced by 1.2 million apps in the iTunes App Store alone.[3]

What no one could have predicted at the time was the long-term effects this *new* industrial revolution would have on our relationships, our time, and, most importantly, our souls. No one could have possibly known that in spite of all this technology enabling us to be more connected and more available than ever before, we would end up feeling lonelier and less present than ever before. Most of us would agree with that basic sentiment, but few of us are willing to do anything about it.

Information Overload

Forty-five minutes of my life that I can never get back. That's how I often feel when I log off Facebook, having engaged in a session of newsfeed mental whiplash. As if it's not overwhelming enough to absorb the tiny micro-bits of information offered in our friends' status updates, now we also have to weed through the landfill of links that promise to enrich our lives with one click. The latest marriage proposal to go viral on YouTube. The hipster mom and dad singing songs from *Frozen* in their minivan. Twenty ways we can use Coca-Cola to clean, brighten, and remove stains. Ten things wives want to hear from their husbands. A warning to avoid the sugarless gummy bears. (Don't ask, but if you're looking for a quick laugh, Google it.) More than 101 household tips for every room in your home. A quiz: "How many Southern phrases do you know?" (For the record, I know fourteen out of sixteen!) Eleven deadly mistakes we didn't know we were making. And seventy-two time-saving tricks. (Funny, "log off Facebook" was not on the list.)

Ignoring the videos and article links takes discipline when you see a running tally of your friends' "likes" and play-by-play comments. Not only that, but each article or video link offers a host of *other* links that provide "related" news or clips encouraging a dozen or more bunny trails to steal your time. Facebook and social media sites are not the only guilty parties bidding for your valuable attention. Do you want to catch up on the latest national news and current events? No problem. Just a few decades ago you had to wait until the evening news offered by the three or four channels on your television set or tune in to your favorite radio news station to find out what had happened that day. Or you could peruse the local newspaper that landed on your doorstep each morning. Now you can access news online at any moment, or if you're *old-school*, you can tune into any number of twenty-four-hour news shows offered on cable and satellite TV. No matter how you access your information, forget about focusing on one story at a time because delivering the news has turned into a three-ring circus with scrolling banners and weather tickers, and if you are viewing it online, add side links with related news (as well as ads featuring products that have been hand-picked based on your past buying patterns). If you weren't suffering from ADHD before, you will after becoming accustomed to the constant influx of information.

The volume of information you can come in contact with on a daily basis is staggering. To give you a bit of perspective, consider that a single edition of the *New York Times* contains more information than a seventeenth-century British citizen would encounter in a lifetime.[4] In his book *In Search of Balance*, author Dr. Richard Swenson noted,

> This modern 250-year segment of time has witnessed more change and progress than all previous millennia combined. Much more. More has happened to more people, more has been learned and earned, more has been discovered and taught, more has been piled up and piled on—more mobility, more media, more work, more technology, more education, more information, more travel, more communications, more weaponry, more possessions, more speed, more of everything.[5]

Perhaps, more really is *less*.

Everywhere we turn, we encounter limitless opportunities that distract us from more important matters. Case in point: Right after I typed the last sentence in the previous paragraph, I took a short break to walk the dogs. Upon my return, I opened my laptop to resume my writing. I decided to hop online quickly and check my e-mail first. Key word: *quickly.* I drafted two replies to e-mails in need of my attention and pressed Send. Then I scanned an e-mail notifying me of a current sales promotion offered by one of my favorite retailers. And this is where I took a wrong turn. I got sucked in by a highlighted promotion: "An Orderly Approach— Storage to Organize Your Master Closet." The article included several thumbnail pictures of the most wonderful master closets I'd ever laid eyes on. If my master closet looked like the ones in the pictures, I'd move in permanently and never come out. I could actually see the floors in these closets because the shoes were filed neatly in acrylic shoeboxes stacked in perfect symmetry along one wall. One of the closets even featured a crystal chandelier centered over a round, tufted ottoman because, hey, why not? Who doesn't want a chandelier and an ottoman in her master closet? Never mind that I'd need to knock down a wall and expand my closet into my son's old bedroom in order to pull off this look, but a girl can dream, right?

Twenty minutes later I *finally* turned my attention back to this chapter to continue writing about the problem of information overload and how it divides our attention. Talk about ironic. My point? The allure of technology is subtle. Many of us have never stopped to consider the powerful appeal of technology and, more frightening, how we have tethered ourselves to the devices that imperceptibly steal our time and attention. That is until now.

Side Effects May Include . . .

In an article from *The New Yorker* titled "How Facebook Makes Us Unhappy," psychologist Timothy Wilson, who has conducted ongoing research related to the emotional impact of social media, noted that college students start going "crazy" after just a few minutes in a room without their phones or computers. "One would think we could spend the time mentally entertaining ourselves," he said. "But we can't. We've forgotten how." The article goes on to conclude that we are "forgetting the path to proper, fulfilling engagement," and Facebook is not the problem but, rather, a symptom.[6]

In spite of a multitude of studies linking excessive time on electronic devices and social media to increased loneliness, depression, anxiety, envy, low self-esteem, and an overall negative impact on mental health, we can't seem to pull ourselves away to find other "paths to proper, fulfilling engagement." That's the problem. As long as we tether our souls to things that cannot deliver true satisfaction and fulfillment, we will always be left wanting something more. The only way to untie the tether is to admit that "more" cannot be found by repeating the same pattern. If technology hasn't delivered the fulfillment we crave by now, it won't ever bring serenity—ever. It's as simple as that.

I am not suggesting we all give up our electronic devices and abstain from all social media. I love my laptop, smartphone, tablet, and all various venues of social media. But I tend to love them more when I use them *in moderation*. And trust me, I've learned this the hard way. So what *exactly* is too much?

You might be too tethered if:

- You take your phone to the bathroom with you.
- You sleep with your phone in the bed with you.
- The *first* thing you do every morning is check your phone, tablet, et al. for any personal messages you might have missed.
- During your nonbusiness waking hours, your phone stays within a five-foot radius of you.
- You feel a compulsive urge to check your phone for personal text messages or other notifications throughout the day.
- You devote excessive amounts of time to social media each day.
- You check one or more of your social media accounts multiple times throughout the day.
- You check your e-mail multiple times a day outside of work hours.
- The thought of not accessing social media or your e-mail for an entire weekend leaves you feeling anxious.
- You could not enjoy a night out without your phone.
- You check your phone while in the company of others.
- The thought of not accessing your computer or phone after 6:00 p.m. causes you stress.
- Your phone constantly alerts you of friend requests, comments, tags, e-mails, texts, and other incoming information.
- Others have complained about your cell phone use while having conversations with you.
- You check your phone for messages while driving.
- You text while driving.
- You check your phone for updates while waiting at red lights.
- You keep your phone out on the table while eating at restaurants.

- You can't remember the last time you read a book or thumbed through a magazine.
- You feel an overwhelming compulsion to check your text messages as they come in and reply to them immediately.
- You rarely go thirty minutes or more without checking your phone or e-mail or engaging in social media.
- You often feel empty after heavy use of your devices or social media.

Some people, by nature of their jobs, have to be tethered outside of work hours, and that is understandable. However, most of us are tied to our devices by choice. In his book *Crazy Busy* author Kevin DeYoung wrote, "Many of us are simply overcome—hour after hour, day after day—by the urge to connect online. And as Christians we know that 'whatever overcomes a person, to that he is enslaved' (2 Pet. 2:19)."[7] Maybe we can relate. The pathway from moderation to overuse is a subtle shift, occurring gradually over time. Many of us haven't even noticed. We have been carried along by the tide of technology, never consciously intending for our use to lapse into overindulgence (or addiction).

God wired our hearts for connection, so we can easily fall into the trap of depending on technology and social media to meet that need. However, our hearts need a permanent, fulfilling, soul-enlarging connection—and only God can provide that. The nagging sense of loneliness we feel after over-engaging in technology highlights that need. The Holy Spirit gently nudges and convicts us when our order of affections becomes misappropriated. At the end of the day, nothing else will match the joy and satisfaction that come from connecting to the one true God.

A simple way to determine whether technology has become

too excessive is to ask yourself one question: "What do I crave more: to connect with God or to connect online?" In other words, which one do you anticipate more? The issue boils down to the order of your affections. Where does God rank among your affections? You can easily *say* He is your primary affection, but do your actions back it up? If media consumption supersedes your relationship with the Lord, you are wading in dangerous waters.

Our relationship with God is not the only relationship that suffers when we overindulge in technology. We also miss out on the blessing of real-life relationships—connections steeped in quality, focused, intentional interaction. Sadly, we live in a culture that prioritizes *Keeping Up with the Kardashians* more than keeping up with our family and friends. When we turn to our devices and social media to "connect," we fail to be present in the relationships that matter most. Eye contact, human touch, the sound of one's voice, and a warm smile cannot be replaced by a text message punctuated by a silly emoticon or a simple "LOL." No doubt technology affords us a greater opportunity to stay in touch with our close friends and family, but it cannot replace real, live interaction.

We've all felt the sting of a misunderstood text, e-mail, or quickly typed reply. Relationships develop over time and require some uninterrupted attention in order to take root and grow. Chances are we all can think of someone who has experienced fallout when a spouse pays more attention to connecting online (Facebook romances, pornography, and inappropriate texts, for instance) than connecting with his or her significant other.

In addition to costing us the blessing of real-life relationships with God, family, and close friends, overindulgence in media consumption can also rob us of spiritual nourishment and encouragement. Hebrews 10:24–25 reminds us, "And let us consider how to stir up one another to love and good works, not neglecting to meet together, as is the habit of some, but encouraging one another, and all the more as you see the Day drawing near." When I read those verses, they immediately bring to mind my Sunday morning Adult Bible Fellowship (ABF) that precedes our Sunday morning worship service. We unpack God's Word together and share wisdom and insight in a way that cannot be duplicated electronically. We share praises and prayer requests and celebrate new births, career changes, birthdays, and other life events. Just as important, we support one another in times of need—a death, a lost job, a miscarriage, depression, financial woes. Whether it involves a hot meal or a listening ear, stirring up one another to love and good works requires being *fully* present and available.

Whether your church offers a Sunday morning Bible study class or a weekly community group, I encourage you to attend one faithfully and make it a priority in your life. If you are struggling to find a church that meets your family's needs, keep looking, and, whatever you do, *don't give up*. The more connected you become to your gadgets and social media, the more critical the need to connect face-to-face with like-minded believers on a regular basis. For the sake of your soul, don't neglect to meet together. And when you do, put your phones away. In fact, turn them off. Yes, shut them off completely. Take an actual, physical, make-notes-in-the-margin Bible. Your soul (and your eyes) needs time away from a screen.

A New and Improved Data Plan

When I think about the word *tethered*, I picture my neighbor's dog that hates being indoors. Regardless of the temperature (and trust me, it can get *hot* in Texas), Annie whines at the door to go outside.

To keep her from running away, my neighbor tethers Annie to a twenty-foot rope clipped to her collar and attached on the other end to a stake in the ground. Annie's world consists of a twenty-foot radius outside the front door, and she seems perfectly content with the arrangement.

In a lot of ways Annie's world mirrors our own when we tether ourselves to technology. Ironically, *we* drove the stake into the ground. The World Wide Web can never replace the real world that awaits us in the expanse beyond our devices, but we must be willing to look up from technology to notice it. At the end of the day, we must determine we are no longer content with our current circumstances in order to see change. We must come to the conclusion that as long as we choose to remain tethered, we will crave true freedom and rest in our souls.

Romans 6:16 cautions, "Don't you realize that you become the slave of whatever you choose to obey?" (NLT). Technology is wonderful, but it was intended to *serve* you, not *master* you. Do you allow your electronic gadgets and social media to call the shots? Do you respond to every chime, notification, and impulse to engage? Or do you set limits to ensure they are serving you and not the other way around?

Here is a revolutionary (and freeing) thought: You don't *have* to answer every phone call. You don't *have* to answer every text within seconds of receiving it. You *can* untether yourself from their grip, but you must be willing to walk away. The common denominator shared by your electronic devices and social media is that they all can be turned off, put away, or shut down. I'm not suggesting you revert back to the days of landlines and handwritten notes (although those are much more personal than a text or an e-mail). However, you *do* need to determine the kinds of technology that enrich your life and get rid of the rest. You need to go on a media diet of sorts by giving up the digital junk food that takes a toll on your soul.

I have learned to recognize the signs that indicate my media consumption is in excess. I also know I tend to fill the time gaps with quick solutions like Facebook, Instagram, texting, online shopping, or hanging out on my favorite news sites. I have to guard vigilantly against excess by establishing self-imposed boundaries. Here is what my new and improved data plan looks like in my own life:

- Rather than posting on several different social media platforms, I mainly use one that automatically feeds into the others without my logging on.
- Currently, I get on Facebook only two days a week, and on each of those days, I spend no longer than twenty minutes. This cuts down on diversions, like clicking interesting links and funny videos. If I see a link I want to click, I save it for later when I have a break or spare time.
- I try to put my phone away when I'm working or spending time with family or friends.
- I go on walks without my phone.
- I try to close my laptop in the evenings to spend time with my husband or engage in a hobby.
- I try to limit my favorite TV shows to a handful.
- Rather than check my text messages as I receive them, I try to let a span of time pass before I read them.
- I'm a news junkie, and I realized I was going to my favorite online news site several times a day, in addition to listening each evening to the local news (at both 6:00 p.m. and

10:00 p.m.) and the national news. Now I check the news online for only five to ten minutes in the morning and watch a televised local newscast and one national newscast in the evening.

- I receive no notifications on my phone other than severe weather alerts (which are rare).
- I receive no social media notifications or e-mails indicating friend requests, comments, and so forth.
- I rarely (except when traveling) access e-mail or social media on my phone.
- When I'm writing, I completely close my Internet browser so I'm not tempted to hop onto my favorite sites.
- When I'm shopping for something online or looking for ideas for a new project, I set a timer on my phone for a reasonable amount of time and make a decision within that time frame.

Keep in mind that this is what works for me—and I'm constantly making adjustments along the way. Your boundaries and guidelines might look different. It's been amazing to see how much time I've redeemed, precious time I can devote to more important matters. I *finally* feel like I have gained some level of control over my digital life, and *I* am the one calling the shots on the amount of time I spend on media consumption. The biggest benefit I've experienced is the peace I feel in my soul. Without the constant distractions, I hear from God more clearly and can spend more uninterrupted and undistracted time with Him throughout my day. In a way, I'm training myself to turn to Him as often as I used to turn to my gadgets, and, as a result, my spiritual life has been recharged.

While your data plan may look differently than mine, I encourage you to determine what might work for you. The important thing is that you make sure technology is serving you, rather than the other way around. It is meant to accentuate your life, not dominate it. You don't have to be tethered any longer. Come up with a new data plan, and set your soul free. There is a world to enjoy right at your fingertips.

Rest Stop

1. When it comes to media consumption, what are your top three distractions? Do they prohibit you from being fully present to those you love?

2. How have you been impacted by the problem of "information overload"?

3. After reading over the list of signs that you may be too tethered (pages 62–63), which ones indicate that you might need to evaluate whether you have a problem with being over-connected? Or do you feel comfortable with the current level of your technology usage?

4. Do you feel a compulsion to engage with your electronic devices or social media? Do you often feel a tangible emptiness in your soul after overindulging?

5. In what ways have you relied on your gadgets or social media to meet your need for connection? Comparatively, how often do you seek connection with God, family and friends, and other believers? Be specific.

The Intervention

1. How has your soul been negatively impacted by being too tethered to your electronic devices and social media? Be specific.

2. Remember, lasting change begins with sincere repentance. The Bible reminds us, "Repent therefore, and turn back, that your sins may be blotted out, that times of refreshing may come from the presence of the Lord" (Acts 3:19–20).

   Recall that the Greek word for "repent" is *mĕtanŏĕō*, and it means "to think differently" or "reconsider."[8] Spend some time in prayer. If you feel that repentance is in order and sincerely desire to "think differently," express that to God.

3. Describe how you "think differently" about your level of media consumption now.

4

Worried Sick

"Don't worry, be happy!"

I let out a heavy sigh and rolled my eyes when I pulled up to the intersection and saw those words on the bumper sticker on the car in front of me. Clearly the driver didn't have a twenty-one-year-old son who had just texted the day before to announce that he and a couple of his college buddies were going to take a spur-of-the-moment, thirteen-hour, all-night road trip to an out-of-town football game in another state. And, as if that wasn't dangerous enough, they were going to head back home less than twenty-four hours after their arrival, with very little sleep to sustain them over the next thirteen-hour leg of their journey home. When I called him to ~~calmly share my concerns~~ yell at him and remind him that the frontal lobe of his brain still had not fully developed, he didn't take it so well. I might have gone too far when I told him that God had appointed me to be his frontal lobe until his brain was fully developed and he was able to make wise choices. Or until he got married, whichever came first. At that point, his wife could take over where I left off. He *might* have even called me a "helicopter mom" before he hung up on me. While I'll admit that the title is sometimes well-earned, I felt my hovering was justified in this particular situation.

What my son didn't realize was that within sixty seconds of reading his text, I had already drummed up a mental picture in my mind of a police officer showing up on my front doorstep to inform me of an accident. My worries had hopped on a runaway train and had taken me along for the ride. Seeing the bumper sticker only rubbed salt in my still-fresh wound. Was it really that easy for some people to shake off worry? Could they wish it away with a fake smile and manufactured euphoria? How could they *not* get caught up in a whirlwind of what-ifs and worst-case conclusions? My son ended up not taking the trip (thanks to a calmer intervention on the part of my husband), but, in the meantime, I spent thirty-six hours in a state of hysteria.

If you've experienced that brand of worry, you know it takes a physical toll on you. Chronic worry or stress sets off an impulsive fight-or-flight reaction that can impact a person's blood pressure and heart rate, among other consequences to the body. According to PsychologyToday.com, worry can lead to an increased risk of heart disease, a depressed immune system, digestive disorder, depression, and memory impairment.[1]

It's normal to worry or stress over certain events. In fact, at low levels, stress can be productive, especially if it serves as motivation to follow through with a necessary action (make a deadline, apply for a new job, schedule a doctor appointment, and so on). The problem is most of us don't know how to turn off the valve of worry and stress. We forget we have a switch. If one situation resolves itself, another one waits in the wings to trigger the next round of worry. Living in worry is all we know. Worrying becomes as natural to us as breathing. Over time, our souls take a beating when we are constantly weighed down with worry. At the core, our worrying reveals a spiritual problem. Managing the emotional or physical symptoms of worrying without addressing the root of the problem will only offer a temporary fix.

Fortunately we have a solution. The Great Physician bids us, "Come to me, all who labor and are heavy laden, and I will give you rest" (Matt. 11:28). We will not experience true rest in our souls until we accept His invitation to lay our troubles at His feet. Jesus carried the weight of our burdens and worries to the cross long ago, but it's up to us to leave them there.

Borrowing Trouble

It is called a "brain-eating amoeba," and I was convinced my youngest son was infected with it. Don't laugh. It's a real thing. The formal name for it is *Naegleria fowleri*, and it lives in untreated swimming pools and untreated well water; it's also found in mud-puddles, ponds, and warm lakes,[2] like the lakes we have in Texas, where the water can heat up to the low eighties in the late summer months. The amoeba finds its way to the brain via the nasal passages, most often by way of water sports (skiing, jet skiing, knee-boarding, for example) or dunking, since water is often forced into the nose at a strong force in these activities. The symptoms appear approximately two weeks after the event, and once they do, death usually occurs within three to seven days. Only a few people have survived a brain-eating amoeba.

I became convinced my youngest son had it after watching my local news station one evening when my son was about fourteen years old. It reported that a twelve-year-old boy had just died of the brain-eating amoeba contracted during his stay at a popular summer camp while knee-boarding at a nearby local lake. A lake, mind you, where we own a house and spend just about every weekend of the summer. *Yes, the very same lake.* And then it hit me. We had just been on the lake the weekend before. We had anchored the boat at a favorite shallow spot right across from the same summer camp where the young boy was infected with the amoeba. *Yes, the very same summer camp.* Oh, and did I mention that the amoeba thrives in warm, *shallow* water?

Before the news reporter had finished reporting on the story, I had plugged "brain-eating amoeba" into Google and pulled it up on WebMD. That's when I read the part about how it travels up the nasal passage. And I remembered my husband and sons throwing the football in the shallow water. *What are the odds?* I asked myself. So, like any well-informed mother, I asked each one if he had gotten any water in his nose while throwing the football in the amoeba-infested lake water over the past weekend. My husband and oldest son assured me they had not . . . after they teased me about my latest worry *du jour.* I had begun to relax until I tracked down my youngest son and asked him if he had gotten any water in his nose. And that's when my heart stopped. "Yeah, I dove for the football a few times, and water shot up my nose once." Jesus, take the wheel.

Over the next few days I became an authority on the symptoms caused by the brain-eating amoeba. I also found a hospital that had treated one of the few survivors because, well, a mother can never be too prepared. When we reached the window of time in which the symptoms would begin to manifest, I told my son to be on guard and instructed him to notify me *immediately* if he experienced a single symptom—headache, fever, stiff neck, vomiting, or (in some cases) hallucinations. I may or may not have texted him while he was at school and asked him if he had a headache. Every day. For a week. He may or may not have taunted me with reports of strange hallucinations, like seeing a unicorn run by one afternoon. I grounded him for that one.

Now that I reflect back on the brain-eating amoeba episode, I am willing to admit that I *may* have gone a *little* overboard. Especially when you consider that only zero to eight people die each year from the amoeba. And this is the problem with worry.

Oftentimes we suffer from a skewed perception gap in which our level of worry far exceeds the odds of the perceived outcome becoming a reality. The truth is my son was at far greater risk of being struck and killed by lightning (approximately fifty deaths in the United States each year),[3] dying from a bee sting (around fifty-four deaths a year),[4] or being mauled to death by a dog (about twenty-six deaths per year).[5] Why didn't I just ban him from the outdoors, where lightning strikes, bees sting, and dogs attack?

Isn't that the case with so many of our burdens and worries? Most of the time, what we worry about never comes to fruition.

In Matthew 6, Jesus offered wise counsel to those who are anxious or have a tendency to worry:

> "Therefore I tell you, do not worry about your life, what you will eat or drink; or about your body, what you will wear. Is not life more than food, and the body more than clothes? Look at the birds of the air; they do not sow or reap or store away in barns, and yet your heavenly Father feeds them. Are you not much more valuable than they? Can any one of you by worrying add a single hour to your life?

And why do you worry about clothes? See how the flowers of the field grow. They do not labor or spin. Yet I tell you that not even Solomon in all his splendor was dressed like one of these. If that is how God clothes the grass of the field, which is here today and tomorrow is thrown into the fire, will he not much more clothe you— you of little faith? So do not worry, saying, 'What shall we eat?' or 'What shall we drink?' or 'What shall we wear?' For the pagans run after all these things, and your heavenly Father knows that you need them. But seek first his kingdom and his righteousness, and all these things will be given to you as well. Therefore do not worry about tomorrow, for tomorrow will worry about itself. Each day has enough trouble of its own." (vv. 25–34 NIV)

"Can any one of you by worrying add a single hour to your life?" In fact, we lose precious hours we can never get back. Hours that would be better spent enjoying the life we have been given and focusing on *what is* rather than *what might be*. I've heard the quote, "Worry does not take away tomorrow's troubles; it takes away today's peace."[6] Worry has no value. Why, then, are we experts at it? Many of us would win medals if worrying were an Olympic sport.

In the passage, Jesus addressed our worrying over legitimate concerns like the basic essentials—food, water, and clothing—and not brain-eating amoebas, Ebola, cancer, freak accidents, financial difficulties, unemployment, prodigal children, global warming, or _____ (fill in the blank with your worry of the week). Jesus was not suggesting that we will be exempt from the difficulties of life but, rather, that He has our backs. He is ultimately in control. He pointed to the evidence: the birds of the air and the flowers of the field. They do not "labor or spin." It dawns on me that when we "spin" out of control with worries of the day, we are stuck in the same place, unable to move forward.

If you and I want to find rest for our souls, we must first acknowledge that when we worry, we are refusing to recognize that God is ultimately in control. At the core, worry boils down to a matter of trust. Do we *really* trust God in any and every situation? I am not suggesting that we throw all caution to the wind and let our kids run around the house with sharp knives. Rather, we should take action to address the source of our worry *and* trust God. We should aim for a healthy balance. When we spend an inordinate amount of time worrying over a situation that ultimately lies outside of our control, we are basically saying, "God, I'm not sure You can handle this one, so move over, I'm in charge." The apostle Peter reminded us, "Cast all your anxiety on him because he cares for you" (1 Pet. 5:7 NIV). The Greek word for "cast" is *ĕpirrhiptō*, and it means literally "to throw upon" or "to cast upon."[7] God bids us to throw, heave, toss, and cast our burdens and worries on Him, but this won't be possible unless we loosen our grips and let go. The choice is simple: hang on or hand them over.

Peace of Me

It's probably not a coincidence that while writing this chapter, I've been in a spin cycle of worry over a situation that lies *completely* outside of my control. There is no planned timetable for resolution or an outcome. An answer could come tomorrow. Or next month. Or in a year. Or several years. Or never. Indefinite limbo. I liken it to sitting in God's waiting room. I don't do uncertainty very well. I like to know the plan, and when the plan fails to unfold in the way I have imagined, I struggle to make sense of it all.

While the outcome of this situation doesn't affect me directly, it seriously affects someone dear to me, so I feel a great deal of pressure to be an example of unwavering faith in the midst of the uncertain outcome. The truth is on some days my faith wavers, and worry makes itself at home. I entertain the what-ifs. I desperately want to fix it. I do my own research on the problem to find a solution hiding out there in cyberspace. One minute I feel hope. The next minute I feel deflated. I despair. Wring my hands. Bite my nails. Lose my appetite. Sigh in frustration. (Grab for the ice cream.) And sometimes I doubt God. Is He really there? Does He even *care* about the situation? Why would He allow such circumstances to someone who loves Him?

When I find myself in that place (again), where doubts are high and trust is low, I eventually cry out to God (again). I beg for peace of mind and rest in my soul. In John 14:27, Jesus said, "I am leaving you with a gift—peace of mind and heart. And the peace I give is a gift the world cannot give. So don't be troubled or afraid" (NLT). The Greek word for "troubled" is *tarassō*, and it means "to stir or agitate."[8] Think of the stomach being in a state of constant agitation. Pass me the Tums, please. Yet Jesus left a gift to rescue us from the spin cycle of worry—His peace. We cannot conjure up that kind of peace, no matter how hard we try or how tightly we grip. Only by letting go and trusting God will we experience the gift of peace. The Greek word for "peace" is *ĕirēnē*, and it means "quietness, rest."[9] The rest we long for in our souls will elude us when we cling to our worries and what-ifs.

How, then, do we gain this peace? How do we maintain it? Philippians 4 holds the answer: "Do not be anxious about anything, but in every situation, by prayer and petition, with thanksgiving, present your requests to God. And the peace of God, which transcends all understanding, will guard your hearts and your minds in Christ Jesus" (vv. 6–7 NIV).

Remember it this way: Peace = Prayer + Petition + Praise.

The Message translates the verses as: "Don't fret or worry. Instead of worrying, pray. Let petitions and praises shape your worries into prayers, letting God know your concerns. Before you know it, a sense of God's wholeness, everything coming together for good, will come and settle you down. It's wonderful what happens when Christ displaces worry at the center of your life."

I love this: "Let petitions and praises shape your worries into prayers, letting God know your concerns." This is the path we need to take. When we get caught up in a spin cycle of worry, we can immediately turn to prayer. We can transform our worries into a prayer wrapped up in a spirit of thanksgiving. When we conclude our prayer with a bookend of praise, we end on a positive, upbeat note of trust in a sovereign and loving God. We praise God for His omniscience because although we don't see the answers or understand the outcomes, He already knows the end from the beginning (Isa. 46:10). We praise God for His sovereignty because even though we lack control over the conclusion, He sits unshaken on His throne (Ps. 47:8). We praise God for His gift of peace that can be ours for the asking. We present our petitions to Him, and we pray, "Your will be done" (Matt. 6:10) because His will is our ultimate desire. And then we leave our worries with Him in His care.

We do this over and over again, *every* time we begin to worry, even when we don't feel like it. The more we practice the discipline of

Prayer + Petition + Praise, the more likely this attitude of submission and trust will become second nature to us when we find ourselves struggling with worry. If we want to break a bad habit, we must substitute the old habit with a new behavior. And what better discipline than one that promises the gift of peace? Peace that can be ours the moment we relinquish control (which we don't really have) and remember that God holds the future in His hands anyway.

Even Though

"I never imagined I would reach forty years old and still be single." A woman at an event shared her heartfelt confession. "From the time I was a little girl, my biggest dream was to be a wife and mother. I never imagined I might not get my dream until I turned thirty and realized the clock was ticking. I've spent my thirties in a constant state of worry that my worst fears might be realized. And now, here I am ten years later, smack-dab in the middle of the worst-case scenario I have feared. Even if I do eventually meet the right guy and get married, chances are it will be too late to have children. So much for my happily-ever-after."

What do you say in response to that kind of deep heartbreak? The last thing this woman needed was some random speaker lady giving her a pep talk to, "Pray harder. It'll all work out!" Nor did she need me to reel off Bible verses and tell her to "count it all joy" in the midst of her broken dreams (James 1:2). Chances are she'd heard the trite clichés countless times before from well-meaning Christians, most of whom were probably already married. The painful truth is this: life doesn't always play out according to the script we have written for ourselves—even though we love Jesus. Sometimes no matter how much we love God, how hard we pray, or how many Bible verses we memorize to assuage our doubts, our worst fears become reality, sending our faith reeling and our questions flying toward heaven.

What do you do when you find yourself with your dreams in pieces and your hope crushed? How do you recover from the heartache without adopting a skewed perspective about life? Is it possible to keep your heart open toward God even when all evidence seems to indicate that He has broken it? Habakkuk, an Old Testament prophet, experienced the agony of unanswered questions and worst-case scenarios. He offered a faith-filled response in the midst of heartbreak and adversity that is still timely for us today. See if you can detect the scenario he was concerned about in the passage that follows:

> O LORD, how long shall I cry for help,
>   and you will not hear?
> Or cry to you "Violence!"
>   and you will not save?
> Why do you make me see iniquity,
>   and why do you idly look at wrong?
> Destruction and violence are before me;
>   strife and contention arise.
> So the law is paralyzed,
>   and justice never goes forth.
> For the wicked surround the righteous;
>   so justice goes forth perverted. (Hab. 1:2–4)

Let me set the stage for you. Habakkuk prophesied about the Babylonian invasion of Judah. The book opens with the prophet lamenting the violence and injustice during King Jehoiakim's reign. Jehoiakim's father, Josiah, had been a good and God-fearing king, but his son did not follow in Josiah's footsteps. It seems like a reasonable question, one you and I might ask of God today. *How long will You allow evil to endure in our country, God? Please do something!*

For me personally, these opening verses bring comfort because they show that God can handle our complaints and questions when they are couched in a humble desire to seek His guidance and comfort. When Habakkuk made his appeal, he asked many of the same questions we, too, ask when faced with disappointing circumstances that are outside of our control. *God, have You left me?* ("O Lord, how long shall I cry for help?") *Why are You allowing this in my life?* ("Why do you make me see iniquity?") *It's not fair!* ("Why do you look idly at wrong?")

After taking his complaint before God, he waited for a reply. The good news is that God could bear the weight of Habakkuk's questions. Unfortunately God's plan for judging the sinful nation would involve the worst-case scenario Habakkuk could have ever imagined:

> "Look among the nations, and see;
>> wonder and be astounded.
> For I am doing a work in your days
>> that you would not believe if told.
> For behold, I am raising up the Chaldeans,
>> that bitter and hasty nation,
> who march through the breadth of the earth,
>> to seize dwellings not their own." (Hab. 1:5–6)

This definitely was *not* the way Habakkuk wanted God to fix the problem. It wasn't the script or happy ending Habakkuk had imagined. God would indeed judge the evil in Judah, but He would use the Chaldeans (the Babylonians) to do it. Let me put this in perspective. Having the Babylonians judge Judah for her sin would be like having ISIS (Islamic State in Iraq and Syria) bring judgment on America. God would use people even more wicked than Judah to judge Judah for her wickedness.

Um, God, is there a Plan B?

The situation was outside of Habakkuk's control, and there was absolutely nothing he could do to change the circumstances. Sound like any situation in your life? Habakkuk had a choice to make. Upon hearing the bad news, he could pout, fume, and rail against God. He could get caught up in the spin cycle of worry, robbing his soul of peace and rest. Or he could continue to trust in God even when His plan didn't make sense. In the final chapter of Habakkuk, we see his amazing response to a worst-case scenario. The chapter begins with this opening line: "A prayer of Habakkuk the prophet" (3:1). Habakkuk responded to his worries and what-ifs with prayer. Sound familiar? He let petitions and praises shape his worries into prayers, letting God know his concerns. Peace = Prayer + Petition + Praise. In fact, the book of Habakkuk closes with an amazing declaration of trust in spite of a worst-case scenario:

> Even though the fig trees have no blossoms,
>> and there are no grapes on the vines;
> even though the olive crop fails,
>> and the fields lie empty and barren;
> even though the flocks die in the fields,
>> and the cattle barns are empty,
> yet I will rejoice in the LORD!
> I will be joyful in the God of my salvation!
> The Sovereign LORD is my strength! (Hab. 3:17–19 NLT)

One Bible commentary notes,

> Habakkuk did not state that he would merely endure in the hour of distress. He said he would rejoice in the LORD and be joyful. God is the inexhaustible source and infinite supply of joy. . . . Far too many people keep trying to buy joy, but happiness is not found in circumstances. Joy is available to everyone, even to those stripped of every material possession, for joy is to be found in a Person. It comes through an intimate and personal relationship with the Lord, so that even those in the worst circumstances can smile.[10]

"Happiness is not found in circumstances." Stop and think about that for a minute. Do you believe that? Imagine the steady peace our souls could enjoy if we decided today that no matter what circumstances life brings our way, we will choose trust and dependence. A worry-free brand of peace. In the classic devotional *My Utmost for His Highest*, Oswald Chambers offered this remedy in times of uncertainty or adversity:

> Notion your mind with the idea that God is there. If once the mind is notioned along that line, then when you are in difficulties it is as easy as breathing to remember—Why, my Father knows all about it! It is not an effort, it comes naturally when perplexities press. Before, you used to go to this person and that, but now the notion of the Divine control is forming so powerfully in you that you go to God about it.[11]

At the close of one women's event, where I shared Habakkuk's amazing declaration, I encouraged the women to write down their list of complaints or circumstances that had interrupted their happiness. I then challenged them to write "Even though" at the top of their lists and at the bottom of their lists to write, ". . . yet I will rejoice in the Lord! I will be joyful in the God of my salvation! The Sovereign Lord is my strength!"

I felt led to give them the opportunity to come up to the microphone and make their declaration of praise to God public. What happened next tops my list of divine, God-sized moments experienced in all my years of serving at events. Trust me, the fact that God prompted me to offer the mic to the audience was proof enough He was in charge. I don't usually take that sort of risk, especially in an audience of 1,500-plus women. I prayed, and then I sat down. For the next half hour women shared their personal "even though" situations:

Even though . . . my husband left me just weeks ago for my best friend . . . yet I will rejoice in the Lord! I will be joyful in the God of my salvation! The Sovereign Lord is my strength!

Even though . . . I've lost my job, my home, and I have no idea how I'm going to pay the bills this month . . . yet I will rejoice in the Lord! I will be joyful in the God of my salvation! The Sovereign Lord is my strength!

Even though . . . I am unable to have children and have undergone disappointment after disappointment in my journey of infertility . . . yet I will rejoice in the Lord! I will be joyful in the God of my salvation! The Sovereign Lord is my strength!

On and on the women kept sharing their declarations of trust. Many choked back tears as they praised God in their personal "even though" circumstances. They mentioned illnesses (many terminal), the deaths of family members (including children), and their struggles with depression, wayward spouses, and prodigal children. There was not a dry eye in the place by the time we finished.

Heartbreaks, broken dreams, and disappointments inevitably come in this fallen world, so it's best to be prepared before the storms roll in. You can't always choose your circumstances, but you can choose your response. Will you trust God even when the money does not come? When the test results come back positive? When you lose your job? When you are betrayed deeply? When the child doesn't return? When God's plan feels like a sick practical joke?

In John 14:1, Jesus declared, "Do not let your hearts be troubled. You believe in God; believe also in me" (NIV). The antidote to worry is trusting in Jesus. The next time you get caught up in the spin cycle of worry, stop yourself and your runaway thoughts. Engage in Prayer + Petition + Praise. No matter what. In any and every situation. Even though. The Sovereign Lord is your strength.

REST STOP

1. On a scale of 1 to 10, with 10 being the most, how much do you struggle with worry? Are you more of a selective worrier or a chronic, full-time worrier? Explain.

2. Do you struggle with a "skewed perception gap" when you worry? Can you think of a time when your level of worry far exceeded the odds of the perceived outcome being realized? Explain.

3. What are some common causes that trigger a spin cycle of worry in your life? Share a recent example when God's peace eluded you. How might it have helped you to employ God's remedy: Peace = Prayer + Petition + Praise?

4. When have you faced an "even though" situation recently? Share an example. If you are experiencing an "even though" situation right now, are you willing to respond with Habakkuk's declaration? If so, write it out:

Even though . . .

. . . yet I will rejoice in the Lord! I will be joyful in the God of my salvation! The Sovereign Lord is my strength!

THE INTERVENTION

1. How has your soul been impacted by the problem of worry? Take a few minutes to think about specific ways worry has taken a toll on your soul and your relationship with the Lord. Write down your thoughts.

2. If worry has been a problem for you, remember that lasting change begins with sincere repentance. Acts 3:19–20 says, "Repent therefore, and turn back, that your sins may be blotted out, that times of refreshing may come from the presence of the Lord."

   Recall that the Greek word for "repent" is *mĕtanŏĕō*, and it means "to think differently" or "reconsider."[12] Spend some time in prayer. If you feel that repentance is in order and you sincerely desire to "think differently," express that to God.

3. Describe how you "think differently" about your struggle with worry now.

PART II

REDEEMING REST

The Recovery

Prioritize the One Thing Needed

Time for God

I was entirely and wholly burned out. When I boarded the flight, the gray and dreary storm clouds matched my mood perfectly. I can't remember a time when I felt more overwhelmed. Deadlines intersected a long list of overcommitments, and I was running on empty. Unfortunately the plane was taking me to another city, to another event to be the keynote speaker, so I had no choice but to strap on my running shoes just a little tighter so I could keep up the pace, exuding calmness and control. Or at least pretending to.

On top of my standard obligations, I had spent the month putting out fires left and right. I had just recently shared with a coworker that I felt as though I was sitting in a tiny, leaky lifeboat in the middle of the ocean, armed with nothing more than a Dixie Cup to dump out the water. I was fighting a losing battle just to stay afloat. The water rose up quicker than I could scoop it out. Something had to change, but I was too overwhelmed to know where to start.

I turned to the window as my eyes filled with tears, thankful I had the row to myself and wasn't forced to engage in the obligatory airplane niceties. How did my life get so busy? As we rose above the clouds and the depressing surroundings, I felt the warmth of the sun hit my face. My weariness welcomed the timely reminder that above the gray and dreary storm clouds, the sun continues to shine. I soaked up the splendor of God's glorious creation for a few more moments before I gave in to the familiar pang of anxious urgency. The short flight would deliver me to my destination too soon, and I wanted to review my message one last time. I pulled out my notes and my Bible from my carry-on, but waves of hypocrisy washed over me as I began to scan my notes. I had no right to lead these women to the throne of God when I failed to make the trek myself on the majority of days. The Spirit clearly nudged me to put away my notes and open my Bible. I had committed to read through the Bible in one year, but I had failed miserably at the plan. My progress was hit or miss—at best.

Desperate for a word from the Lord, I opened up the Scripture to the assigned reading for the day in Psalm 107:

> Others went to sea in ships,
>   conducting trade on the vast waters.
> They saw the LORD's works,
>   His wonderful works in the deep.
> He spoke and raised a tempest
>   that stirred up the waves of the sea.
> Rising up to the sky, sinking down to the depths,

their courage melting away in anguish,
they reeled and staggered like drunken men,
and all their skill was useless. (vv. 23–27 HCSB)

The lifeboat. The Dixie Cup. The waves tossing the boat around in the deep as the water lapped over the edges. Yes, God had gotten my attention. He provided a timely word for me. I must have read it at least a dozen times before my flight landed. I highlighted the phrase: "And all their skill was useless" (v. 27). Nothing unsettles us more than living in a situation beyond our control. If we tend to lapse into fix-it mode as our first line of defense, reading the statement, "and all their skill was useless," can leave us exposed and humbled. And that's a good thing. This passage doesn't recommend *giving up*, but rather *giving in*. Here's what follows:

Then they cried out to the LORD in their trouble,
and He brought them out of their distress.
He stilled the storm to a murmur,
and the waves of the sea were hushed.
They rejoiced when the waves grew quiet.
Then He guided them to the harbor they longed for.
(Ps. 107:28–30 HCSB)

The New International Version renders verse 27 as "they reeled and staggered like drunkards; / they were at their wits' end." Can you relate? We've all experienced our fair share of wit's end moments, but many of us remain stuck in a perpetual state of wit's end. Moments turn to days, and days turn to months. Before long, being at wit's end becomes our standard default setting. Fortunately, you and I don't have to set up camp and live there. We can choose differently. The harbor we long for lies just off in the distance, but many of us have lost sight of the shoreline because we can't see past the waves. We funnel our energy into staying afloat and scooping out the water one Dixie Cup at a time rather than turning to the One who openly rebuked the wind and sea with a simple command: "'Peace! Be still!' And the wind ceased, and there was a great calm" (Mark 4:39).

The harbor provides the "great calm" we deeply crave. I love the story of Jesus' calming the storm because it reminds me that even the disciples—those closest to Jesus and who witnessed firsthand His wonderful works—failed to cry out to Him when the storm overwhelmed them. They were at their wits' end while Jesus slept soundly just a few feet away. Does that ring true of you and me?

It's been years since God met me in my wit's end moment on the plane and led me to that beautiful passage in Psalm 107. That night in the hotel I cried out to Him for relief from the storm, and, true to His character, He calmed the waves. My problems didn't magically melt away, but I could finally see the faint silhouette of a shoreline in the distance. God would guide me safely into the harbor, but I had to admit that my skills, scheming, plans, and back-up plans could not fix my situation. I had to cease striving long enough to acknowledge He is God . . . and I am not (Ps. 46:10). Which begs the question: Why did I settle for a Dixie Cup when I could have turned immediately to the One whom the wind and the seas obey?

Help for Distracted Souls

When I reflect on my season of burnout, I can't help but think of the two sisters, Mary and Martha, in Luke 10, whom we talked about earlier. As we noted, Martha was "distracted with much serving" (v. 40) while Mary "sat at the Lord's feet and listened to his teaching" (v. 39). The passage tells us Martha was frustrated because Mary had left her alone to deal with the dinner preparations. In a way only sisters could do, Martha tattled on her sister to Jesus and made the appeal, "Lord, do you not care that my sister has left me to serve alone? Tell her then to help me" (v. 40). Did you notice her accusatory tone? Her frenzy had skewed her perspective and filtered into her relationships. Can you relate?

Interestingly, the Greek word for "distracted" is *pĕrispaō*, and it means to "drag all around."[1] I imagine most of us can relate to that word picture. What drags you all around and hinders you from sitting at the feet of Jesus?

If verse 40 had been written about you, how might it read?

> But _____ [your name] was distracted with
> much _____ [fill in the blank].

- Volunteering
- Children's extra-curricular activity
- Online shopping
- Attention to appearance
- Attention to fitness and nutrition
- Time spent on Facebook/Instagram/Twitter/Pinterest
- Church work
- Worry over world events
- Attention to career
- Overeating
- Texting
- Home decorating
- Materialism

Martha was looking for two things when she asked Jesus to intervene: physical help and validation for her choice to serve. Never did she imagine Jesus would, instead, defend Mary's position as the more important of the two. He didn't take the bait but looked past the question (which was quite accusatory) to the deeper problem at hand. "Martha, Martha, you are anxious and troubled about many things, but one thing is necessary. Mary has chosen the good portion, which will not be taken away from her" (Luke 10:41–42). He may as well have said, "Martha, Martha, you have become distracted again, but one thing is necessary. Mary has chosen to pursue what matters most, and her soul is at peace. What is more important: feeding your guests or feeding your soul? Need I remind you that I recently fed more than five thousand people with just five loaves and two fish? I can handle feeding this crowd tonight, so put down your oven mitt and come join your sister." Ouch.

Jesus was not making a statement against serving, but rather emphasizing the importance of sitting *before* we serve. When we fail to make time for Jesus, we serve on an empty tank. Martha had allowed busyness to interrupt the one thing needed: time with the Lord. God created our souls for communion with Him. When we rush through our days and fail to make time to sit at the feet of Jesus, we experience unrest in our souls. God wired us for fellowship with Him, and when we forego that fellowship, we feel empty and dissatisfied. We grab His truths on the run and settle for crumbs, whether it's a Sunday-morning sermon our pastor spoon-feeds us or a devotional that lands in our inbox that we end up speed-reading at the same pace we read the Groupon offer that preceded it. But a relationship with Jesus Christ is our richest treasure in this life, a reward that comes at a high cost—our time and our undivided attention. Why do we settle for crumbs when we've been invited to sit at His banquet table and enjoy a feast?

We can scan the bookstore aisles and find dozens of books advising us on the importance of reading our Bibles and praying on a consistent basis. However, most of these books provide a quick-fix, behavior-modification formula to get back on track. Rarely are we challenged to take a deeper look at the problem and examine our hearts to figure out *why* we avoid God or put Him last on our lists. Formulas, reading plans, acronyms, and systems will address only the surface problem and provide surface-level improvement. When Martha tattled to Jesus about her slacker sister, she fully expected Him to intercede on her behalf. Isn't that what we do when we say yes to too much and end up with too much on our plate? We send up a flare prayer for reinforcements to help us *maintain the pace*, never imagining that God wants us to *change the pace*.

Jesus loved Martha enough to offer her insight into the root of her problem: "Martha, Martha, you are anxious and troubled about many things." One Bible commentary notes that in repeating her name, "he speaks as one in earnest, and deeply concerned for her welfare. Those that are *entangled* in the cares of this life are not easily *disentangled*."[2] Jesus knew that unless Martha acknowledged the real distraction that hindered her from sitting at His feet, the pattern of frantic serving and busyness would continue.

What hinders you from settling in to be still with Jesus? Maybe it's not anxiety. Maybe something else captures your time and attention. Whatever the source, your problem won't be solved if you just modify your behavior and sit down because "good Christians spend time with Jesus." Your new regiment might produce short-term change, but you'll likely return to your familiar distractions unless you acknowledge their hold over you.

How might verses 41–42 read if Jesus were addressing you directly, instead of Martha?

"_____, _____ [your name twice], you are
_____, but one thing is necessary."

How might He fill in the last blank?

- Overwhelmed by a never-ending to-do list
- Burdened by shame
- Bound by your past
- Worried about the future
- Enslaved by an ongoing sin
- Depressed
- Brokenhearted
- Bitter
- Feeling hopeless
- Discouraged and confused
- Anxious about your children
- Saddled with debt
- Consumed with being a perfect mother
- Running from your problems
- Desperate for the world's applause
- Worn-out from seeking your worth in the world's approval
- Burned out from doing it all with no relief in sight

Jesus wanted Martha to bring her burdened heart to Him for healing. Sitting at the feet of Jesus was the *one* thing, and Jesus the one Person, she needed. Why, then, was she a no-show? Better yet, why are we no-shows?

The Busyness Trap

Imagine if your to-do list for tomorrow looked like this:

- Teach large crowd at the synagogue
- Cast a demon out of a man possessed by an unclean spirit in the synagogue
- Pay a visit to a friend's home
- After arriving at a friend's home, heal his mother-in-law who is ill with a fever
- Entertain a throng of visitors who show up unexpectedly
- Heal all who are sick among the crowd
- Ditto for those who are demon-possessed
- Call it a day

Most of us would be toast after teaching a large crowd. We'd probably schedule a counseling session after casting out the first demon. Few of us would disagree that a nap (or a long vacation) would be in order by nightfall. Jesus was no stranger to busy, overcrowded days. Yet in this account of a single day in His life, as recorded in Mark 1:21–34, I was struck by one word in particular that appeared four times in the passage.

And they went into Capernaum, and immediately on the Sabbath he entered the synagogue and was teaching. (v. 21)

And immediately there was in their synagogue a man with an unclean spirit. (v. 23)

And immediately he left the synagogue and entered the house of Simon and Andrew, with James and John. (v. 29)

Now Simon's mother-in-law lay ill with a fever, and immediately they told him about her. (v. 30)

Immediately. Just reading the word makes my heart rate spike.
It describes the urgency many of us feel to rush from one activity
to the next, checking off tasks one by one. Jesus experienced hurried and harried days just like we do. Remember, while He lived
on earth in bodily form, He was fully God *and* fully human. He
had the capacity to suffer burnout and exhaustion just like any
other human being. And, like us, He had to make choices each day
about how He would spend His time. If ever a person kept a fully
booked calendar, it was Jesus. Think about it. His mission was "to
proclaim good news to the poor . . . to proclaim freedom for the
prisoners and recovery of sight for the blind, to set the oppressed
free, to proclaim the year of the Lord's favor" (Luke 4:18–19 NIV).
He had three short years to accomplish that purpose. The clock
was ticking. Yet Jesus never demonstrated stress or panic, and He
never exhibited the frenzied pace we see today. Most importantly,
He was never too busy to meet with God. At the top of His to-do
list on the following day, we find: "And rising very early in the
morning, while it was still dark, he departed and went out to a
desolate place, and there he prayed" (Mark 1:35).

Rather than basking in the limelight of His newfound celebrity status, Jesus retreated from the crowd. In fact, one commentary
notes, "He retired that he might escape the applause of men, which
they were ready to lavish upon him after seeing so many miracles."[3]

If anyone could justify hitting the snooze button, Jesus had
that right, especially after enduring such a busy day. Yet He did
just the opposite—He got up earlier than normal. The King James
Version substitutes "still dark" for "a great while before day." I

doubt I would have gotten out of my pj's (except for that counseling appointment). Even if we could match the intensity and pace of His day, I imagine many of us would retreat into a mind-numbing exercise to decompress from the stress of the day. And that's where so many of us take a wrong turn. The place we *should* escape to is the feet of Jesus. He alone can stabilize our souls and recharge our spirits to run the next heat in the race. He understood the necessity of pulling back and retreating to reconnect with the Father. No wonder He commended Mary for choosing the good portion—being at His feet. He had experienced firsthand the benefits of resting in God's presence and listening for His still, quiet voice. He recognized His time with God was an absolute necessity rather than an optional chore on His to-do list.

I don't want us to miss the importance of this passage and the underlying truths we can glean from it. Jesus modeled the kind of rhythm of life that we should emulate. If Jesus needed that precious time alone with God, then why do we think we can forgo it? We were never meant to live at a frazzled and frenzied pace that edges out the one thing needed. If our souls lack rest, a lack of stillness before God is the reason.

The passage in Mark 1 also tells us that Jesus knew how to draw a healthy boundary between His divine assignment and the never-ending demands that pressed in around Him. While He reconnected with the Father, "Simon and those who were with him searched for him, and they found him and said to him, 'Everyone is looking for you'" (Mark 1:36–37).

Of course they were looking for Him. Do you blame them? After witnessing the miracles He had performed the day before, I imagine the whole village was lining up for Round Two, whether the plight was a hangnail or heart disease. But Jesus had a different plan: "And he said to them, 'Let us go on to the next towns, that I may preach there also, for that is why I came out'" (v. 38).

Jesus declined their summons to play the role they had scripted for Him. He moved on to the next village to fulfill the assignment God had given Him for that place at that time. Likely, God gave Him clear direction in that quiet, desolate place, away from the crowds and noise and the lures of applause and praise. His time alone with the Father gave the Son the much-needed fellowship and communion His soul craved. This continual abiding in God allowed Jesus to say with assurance, "I glorified you on earth, having accomplished the work that you gave me to do" (John 17:4). He did what His Father had asked Him to do, and yet Jesus didn't heal every person, perform hundreds of resurrections, or provide food for every hungry crowd. Being alone with God allowed Jesus to keep focused on the ultimate act of service—His sacrificial death on the cross.

I wonder how often we wear ourselves out trying to meet the steady stream of pressing needs around us, when God is trying to grab our attention and say, "Give it a rest and move on, sister!" God never intended you to answer every e-mail, respond to every text, say yes to meet every need, serve on every committee, and then buckle under the weight of an overcrowded calendar. If the busyness trap hinders you from the one thing needed, God is ready to set you free.

Quiet-Time Flunkie

How do you feel when you see or hear the buzz phrase *quiet time*? For a good part of my Christian life, I endured the weight of a low but steady level of guilt because no matter how hard I tried,

I couldn't measure up to the rigid quiet-time blueprint touted by many well-meaning Christian leaders. I own an enviable collection of journals, all of which sit empty or contain text only on the first few pages. I have unopened packages of 3 x 5 note cards (for learning memory verses), highlighter pens, and enough Bible-reading plans and weekly prayer guides to take me into the next century.

When I would hear a persuasive teaching related to what constitutes the "perfect" quiet time, I'd stock up on all the recommended essentials and set my alarm (because every good Christian knows the best time to have a quiet time is in the morning). I'd fly out of the gates strong, running the course with a newfound quiet-time zeal, but by the end of the first week, I'd lag behind the pack and limp along with halfhearted enthusiasm. Before long, I was hitting the snooze on my alarm and retiring the empty journals and blank note cards to the cabinet in my office, where other empty journals and blank note cards live in happy harmony. I was a quiet-time flunkie. I didn't lack commitment to reading my Bible and praying, but I couldn't follow the formula that so many other believers have embraced as a standard discipline.

My husband is a shining example of someone who can maintain a steady and consistent daily quiet time. If you look up *quiet time* in the dictionary, you will find his smiling face with an open Bible in his lap, yellow highlighter in hand, and an old photocopied printout of the characteristics of God (so he can praise God for each one over the course of the month). If I'm a quiet-time flunkie, my husband is a quiet-time overachiever. Never mind that my husband was also a model student and managed to graduate from college (chemical engineering) in *four years* at the top of his class (valedictorian, to be exact). In fact, he scored all *A*s and only one *B* in his entire college career. I scored one *B* as well, but I was rather excited about my *B*. I kid. I may have scored a few more *B*s, but unlike my husband, I viewed a *B* as a grade-point booster, not a grade-point buster.

My husband and I are wired very differently. His personality lends itself to structure, and mine, not so much. For years, though, I berated myself for being unable to live up to the standard quiet-time formula. Even worse, I imagined a God who was tapping on His watch and shaking His head back and forth when I approached His throne. "Oh, it's you again. [Insert heavy sigh.] It's about time you decided to make an appearance. How about we see if you can make it ten minutes without losing your train of thought when the dryer buzzes or your cell phone chimes?" When we view God as an angry taskmaster who is more concerned with our behavior than our hearts, meeting with Him becomes more about maintaining the rules than maintaining the relationship.

When I finally cut myself some slack over my perceived quiet-time failures and realized that God doesn't endorse one particular method for spending time with Him, I felt freedom to seek Him with a sincere heart, not a guilty ambivalence. What works for one person may not work for another. Using a one-year Bible (containing 365 readings with portions from the Old Testament, New Testament, Psalms, and Proverbs) works best for me. When I skip a day (or more), I can often catch up, but sometimes I grant myself grace and pick up on the current day. (I realize this would be very hard for those of you who are perfectionists.) I also bought a Bible software program for my computer, and, if time allows, I love to look up verses that jump off the page while I'm reading the assigned passages. I'll dig deeper to discover the Greek or Hebrew words and definitions for key concepts and read several different commentaries to gain a better insight into the meaning of the verse or passage. I might go three or four days without opening my Bible, only to spend an hour or two the next night dissecting a single passage and poring over resources that will give me further insight.

My prayer life looks more like an ongoing conversation with God throughout the day than a prescribed time each day. I praise Him for His many attributes as I notice them throughout my day, and I take time to savor the moments when I notice His handiwork. Sometimes I listen to a favorite worship playlist of hymns that continually bring me to tears over the beauty of the gospel. I have no idea how long my quiet times last because I meet with Him off and on throughout my day. I have finally found the structure that works best for me (less structure), and I am focused more on building my relationship with Him rather than following a set of rules.

Maybe you clock in faithfully day after day, but do so more out of duty than delight. Rather than viewing your time with God as the one thing needed, it has become "the one thing I'm supposed to do." As a result, your solid track record shows your diligence, but your faith feels stale. Behavior modification tactics rarely yield a sincere and thriving relationship with God. Mary sat at Jesus' feet because she viewed that time as an absolute necessity, not an item to be checked off her to-do list. You can meet with God on a regular and consistent basis and miss Him entirely in the process. In other words, you might be present when the roll is called, but absent when it comes to *hearing* Him.

When you impose rigid guidelines that dictate how your time with God should look, you turn that time into a dreaded chore rather than an anticipated privilege. Let me ask you this question: If you were to skip your time with God, would you be more concerned about missing the mark or missing God? Your answer to that question can offer valuable insight about your underlying motivation for spending time with God. What if you scrap preconceived notions about what constitutes a quiet time and start with a clean slate? One size doesn't fit all when spending time with God.

When we fail to spend time with God on a consistent basis, it's easy to forget who He is and how much He loves us. Disappointments, anger, unconfessed sin, unanswered prayers, unmet expectations, and a variety of other disruptions can leave us feeling alienated from God and tempted to avoid Him. Yet avoiding Him only increases the unrest we feel in our souls because our God created us to find our rest solely in Him.

If you have been avoiding God, I want to encourage you to "with confidence draw near to the throne of grace, that [you] may receive mercy and find grace to help in time of need" (Heb. 4:16). Approach His throne and pour out your heart to Him. If your heart is breaking because of unanswered prayer, *tell* Him. If you are caught up in a web of sin, go to Him and confess it. If you are burdened by your past, ask Him to remind you of His grace that set you free.

The Greek word for "confidence" in this verse is *parrhēsia*, and it means "outspoken-ness, frankness, bluntness."[4] Approach Him and begin the conversation. Tell Him why you've been avoiding Him. He can handle it. Chances are you have imagined God to be someone He's not. It's time to mend the relationship. If you're caught up in a stronghold of sin, restoration may not happen overnight, but it begins with your willingness to approach Him. He has been waiting for you, like the father waiting for his wayward son (Luke 15:20). He is not angry with you. Nor is He sitting on His throne waiting to punish you for your rebellion. You have not exhausted the limit of some arbitrary forgiveness quotient. He does not tire of offering you grace to cover your sin. Again. For the bazillionth time. He won't lecture you for being a no-show, regardless of your reason. He eagerly waits to offer mercy and grace in your time of need.

Regardless of what hinders you from connecting with God, your soul will lack rest until you turn to Him as the one thing needed. Take a few minutes to stop and ponder the glorious mystery that the God of this universe not only stepped in to save you from your sins, but He also wants to know you and wants *you* to know *Him*. Recognizing that astounding truth ought to bring each one of us to our knees in humble gratitude and worship. He does not force Himself into our lives but, instead, gives us the choice. Many of us have become so distracted, and, like Martha, we have failed to see an alternative to our chaotic, frenzied, duty-filled lives. We have been given another choice—a better choice—that will bring rest to our frenzied souls.

Have you chosen the one thing needed? If not, what are you waiting for?

Rest Stop

1. Which of the two sisters do you relate to more: Mary or Martha? If you are a Martha, what distracts you from the one thing needed? (Refer back to pages 101 and 104 and the list of common distractions and deeper issues.) What is your deeper issue?

2. What would it look like for you to go away to a deserted place?

3. How did you answer this question on page 111: "If you were to skip your time with God, would you be more concerned about missing the mark or missing God?" What might this say about your view of God?

4. Could you relate to my story of feeling like a quiet-time flunkie? If so, describe your struggle.

5. What changes (if any) do you feel led to make regarding your plan for spending time with God? In other words, what works for you?

THE ONE-WEEK DARE

Over the next week, I dare you to set aside a block of time every day to sit at the Lord's feet and soak up His Word. Whether you pick a book of the Bible to read or decide to focus on a specific text, allow yourself enough time to meditate on what you read and talk about it with the Lord. If possible, try to meet with Him in the morning in order to set the course for your day. In addition, implement a daily and consistent time of prayer. Remember, prayer is an ongoing conversation, so make it a practice to keep the conversation going each day for one solid week. Specifically, ask God to open your eyes and your heart to what He is teaching you during this time. Even if you are disciplined in your quiet time and prayer time, focus on *building the relationship* rather than *maintaining the ritual*. Don't view it as one more "rule" to bog you down, but rather as a way to get reacquainted with God.

If it's been a while since you've spent time with God, consider making the first day a time in which you commit to "with confidence draw near to the throne of grace" (Heb. 4:16). Remember, the Greek word for *confidence* means "outspokenness, frankness, bluntness." Pour out your heart to Him. If you've been avoiding Him, tell Him why. Begin an honest conversation with Him. If you have been faithful in spending time with God, but your time with Him has become routine and predictable, consider changing an element—a different Bible translation, a different devotional, a worship playlist. Focus on the relationship. Just show up, sit down, and enjoy the one thing needed.

6

Create Room to Breathe

Time for Solitude

When I was ten years old, my grandparents gave me a children's Bible for Christmas. I had never owned a Bible, in spite of the fact that I lived in the Bible Belt, where attending church was viewed by most as being as essential as brushing your teeth. I was one of those "unchurched" kids, who showed up on an occasional Sunday after spending the night with a churchgoing friend. Truth be told, I envied my friends who piled into the family station wagon in their fancy church clothes with their Bibles in hand every Sunday morning. So when my grandparents gave me a Bible to call my own, I felt a bit more connected to the God about whom my friends sometimes talked.

I remember climbing up on my daybed and opening the Bible for the first time. The crisp pages stuck together as I attempted to turn them. I had no idea where to start reading it, but I figured the beginning was a good place since that's where you started with other books. So I began in Genesis. My goal was to read the whole Bible in the hope I would know all about the stories my friends were learning at their churches. I made it through the creation account, the story of Adam and Eve, the fall in the garden, and even the Cain and Abel story. However, when I arrived at the long account of Adam's family tree in chapter 5, I gave up the pursuit after getting lost in a sea of "begats" and hard-to-pronounce names. Even so, throughout my childhood I would still pull out that Bible when I was feeling sad or confused, and I'd read a psalm printed in the front section before the Old Testament began. I reasoned that given its strategic placement, the psalm must be important. My Bible even included a colored caricature of a shepherd boy sitting on a grassy hillside with sheep grazing in the field behind him—a classic illustration of the Twenty-Third Psalm. The shepherd boy didn't look much older than I was, so I concluded the passage must be for kids, and I set out to memorize the psalm. Having that psalm tucked away in my heart brought me comfort and peace over the years.

A little more than a decade later, I came to know the Good Shepherd of the Twenty-Third Psalm, but I didn't feel like I was meeting Him for the first time. Ironically, those first verses I committed to memory as a child would prove to be some of the hardest verses to live out as an adult:

> The LORD is my shepherd,
> I shall not want.
> He makes me lie down in green pastures;
> He leads me beside quiet waters.
> He restores my soul. (vv. 1–3 NASB)

Green pastures. Quiet waters. A soul restored. Where do I sign up? One Bible commentary has this to say about the opening verses of Psalm 23: "God makes his saints to lie down; he gives them quiet and contentment in their own minds, whatever their lot is; their souls dwell at ease in him, and that makes every pasture green."[1] In fact, the Hebrew word for "restore" is *shûwb*, and it means to "retreat, recover, refresh, relieve."[2] This type of soul restoration can be found only in solitude—a foreign concept in our hurried culture today. But if we are to recover from our constant striving and busyness, we must rediscover solitude and make it a steady discipline in our lives.

Going It Alone

When was the last time you enjoyed a time of purposeful solitude? I'm not referring to the moments you snag while sitting in the carpool line or reading a book before bedtime. I'm talking about the type of solitary rest that has no utilitarian purpose other than simply to rest and catch your breath. This kind of solitude is free from the pull of technology, the demands of others, ongoing daily responsibilities, and the constant hum of white noise that threatens to take over your life on a daily basis. In short, a Psalm 23 kind of rest.

Imagine for a moment that you are the shepherd in this psalm. Try to put yourself in the picture. You're lying on a grassy knoll—the soft, golf-course kind of grass. The weather is perfect. The sun warms your face while a gentle breeze tickles the leaves in a cluster of trees nearby. You lie back and fold your arms behind your head, resting comfortably in your interlocked hands. You close your eyes and soak in the moment one second at a time. No laptop, phone, to-do list, or preschooler beckons for your attention. Your calendar is clear, and you're free for the day (we can pretend, right?). You don't need to be anywhere, and, better yet, no one needs you. You are free to relax . . . and breathe . . . and think.

Can you enjoy the solitude, moment by moment? Can you allow the solitude to slow your mind and your emotions? If you're like me, your body may be still, but your mind often fails to get the memo. I might sustain a few minutes of stillness before my mind retreats back to its default setting of mental overdrive:

> *Did I lock the door when I left the house?*
> *Rats, I forgot to move the clothes over from the washer to*
>   *the dryer.*
> *I wonder if one of the kids is trying to call me right now.*
> *Did I ever RSVP to that wedding invitation? Yikes, did I*
>   *even send a gift?*
> *I should be preparing my Bible study.*
> *Gee, this sun is warm. Did I apply sunscreen this morning?*

Why is it so difficult to still our minds? One obvious reason is that technology has afforded us the luxury of staying connected with others at all times, making solitude—real solitude—a rare commodity. However, I believe a bigger factor contributes to the problem: many of us avoid solitude because we associate it with loneliness. To dodge this feeling of aloneness and the negative emotions it evokes, we over-connect, overcommit, and adopt a steady pace of constant overdrive in order to escape the dreaded lull that might occur should we ever slow down. We feed this frenzy because in the quiet solitude, we aren't quite certain who we are. Oh sure, we put up a spiritual front and say we deeply desire more time for rest and solitude, but deep down we fear solitude because it strips us of our titles and roles. Our worth is so destructively connected to our doing, serving, solving, and going that apart from that pace, we might suffer a loss of identity. Yet the very thing we're trying to avoid—solitude—is the very thing that heals our weary souls.

Jesus and Solitude

Jesus knew the importance of solitude. In the sixth chapter of Mark, He sent the twelve disciples out in pairs to preach, cast out demons, and heal people of their illnesses. When they returned from their mission, they learned about the brutal beheading of John the Baptist and laid his body in a tomb. After the disciples gave their report of all they had done on their journeys, Jesus responded to them by calling them away to solitude: "Come away by yourselves to a secluded place and rest a while" (v. 31 NASB). The latter part of the verse explains, "For there were many people coming and going, and they did not even have time to eat" (NASB).

The Greek word for "rest" is *anapauō*, and it means "to refresh."[3] This word is not synonymous with sleep. Nor does this word represent a time devoted to prayer and communion with God. This brand of rest centers on solitude. The only parameters Jesus gave His disciples when He sent them off for a time of rest was to "come away by yourselves" and to retreat "to a secluded place"—not together as a group, but each one alone. Verse 32 tells us, "They went away in the boat to a secluded place by themselves" (NASB). One Bible commentary notes, "Christ calls them to come *themselves apart*; for, if they had anybody with them, they would have something to say, or something to do, for their good; if they must *rest*, they must be *alone*."[4]

Jesus commanded the disciples not only to remove themselves from their immediate circumstances but also to remove themselves from each other. This rest was not intended to be a group activity. Nor was it "leisure rest," which we will discuss in the next chapter. Rather, Jesus instructed them to stop for a solitary, quiet rest, a contemplative rest—a time to reflect, think, and process all they had seen and heard.

Stop and consider the disciples' fragile emotional state upon returning from their journeys. They had come back to Jesus on an emotional high after seeing many miracles take place, yet their spirits had been dampened by the death of John the Baptist. Jesus could have given the disciples a fiery pep talk about the need to persevere in the midst of tough times. Yet Jesus determined that alone time was their most urgent need, so He prescribed solitude to restore their souls. One commentary notes, "He calls them only to rest *awhile*; they must not expect to rest *long*, only to *get breath*, and then to go to work again."[5] The passage doesn't indicate how long the disciples' rest time lasted, but it couldn't have been long because they assisted Jesus with a significant miracle later that evening—feeding five thousand-plus hungry people with five loaves and two fish. No doubt Jesus knew that without rest the disciples would have had nothing but dregs to offer.

Many of us can relate to pouring out from a place of emptiness. Part of our problem is that when our souls are weary (a different kind of weary from what the disciples experienced, but just as valid), we typically avoid the very remedy Jesus prescribed. Rather than "come away by ourselves to a secluded place" where we can think, feel, and ponder the condition of our souls, we seek solace in the very things that quite likely contributed to the problem in the first place. We trade solitude for more busyness. We numb our minds with activities such as watching TV, including twenty-four-hour news and celebrity gossip shows. We trade solitude for a few extra minutes on social media, reading posts from people we've not seen in decades. We forsake solitude so we can juggle extracurricular activities our children won't remember ten years from now. We abandon solitude to respond instantly to our cell phones' every buzz, ding, and chime. Even when we actually come close to engaging in solitude, we sabotage the moment by documenting it on social media by way of a picture, after we find the perfect filter and brainstorm a creative caption. Bottom line? We stink at solitude.

Just What the Doctor Ordered

While thumbing through one of my many vintage magazines, I stumbled upon this interesting counsel in the *Ladies' Home Journal*, September 1894:

> A great nerve doctor, famous in two continents, says that "Every woman whose nervous strength is at all depleted, or whose life is an active one in many directions, should devote a half hour to an hour of every day to absolute rest isolated from all. Her room should be darkened and orders given that she shall not be disturbed, when, with closed eyes and relaxed muscles, she shall lie prostrate, hushing herself to all busy thoughts and cares. . . . Even ten minutes so spent will be a refreshment, and the busiest life may spare that much from its activities, since one is thus made capable of longer endurance.[6]

The article went on to say that the most convincing argument for the doctor's recommended plan of a regular noonday rest was his claim that such rest would "brighten young eyes and retard the dreaded coming of wrinkles to the middle-aged."[7] Ladies, I believe we've stumbled upon the fountain of youth. We should throw out our useless wrinkle creams and crawl into bed when the clock strikes noon! Seriously, what woman would resist the opportunity to be "isolated" in a darkened room with "orders given that she shall not be disturbed"?

I realize this exercise might not be practical for mothers with needy preschoolers or women who work full-time in an office environment and only have a limited amount of time for a break. However, this practice is certainly worth a try, even if for a brief five to ten minutes. And while it may not be practical to take to the bed and hang a Do Not Disturb sign on the door without your kids burning down the house or your friends worrying that you're depressed, you *could* establish a nook in your home as your own personal quiet zone. Find a comfy chair (one you already own or ask for a new one for your birthday). Buy an afghan, a cute throw pillow, and a scented candle to cozy up the space and make it yours.

I have established both a special space indoors and another one out back on my porch (for when the weather is nice). I bought a hummingbird feeder, some wind chimes, and a strand of twinkle lights. As an empty nester, I don't have to contend with many interruptions, but just the act of retreating to my own space helps me mentally shift gears from work mode to rest mode. I sometimes have my quiet times in my quiet-zone space, but I mainly use it as a retreat to catch my breath and practice being still. It has also become my go-to place when I experience writer's block. I leave my phone and laptop behind, and I take nothing with me, except for my little Yorkie who sits faithfully by my side. Even a brief five minutes restores my soul, clears my mind, and gives me enough energy to tackle what remains in my day. Since I started doing this, I have been amazed by how this simple act can make such a difference. I only wish I'd thought of it when my kids were young and I needed it the most.

Try it. Find a quiet corner inside your home (or outside), shuffle the furniture around if need be, and make it clear to your family members that this is *your* space. If you can train your kids not to touch a hot stove, you can train them to leave Mom alone when she's sitting in her quiet zone. If you work full-time, consider finding a spot near your office where you can retreat for a brief break when you need to clear your mind. If you have an office of your own, consider switching from your office work chair to a comfortable chair in a cozy space you create just for this purpose.

Once you establish your quiet-zone space, the remaining tasks are easy. Really! Leave your phone behind or turn it off. Close your laptop or move it out of sight. Turn off all background noise. You can play music as long as it lends to your ability to rest. If you are indoors, dim or turn out the light. Sit back, close your eyes, and clear your mind. For some, you may need five to ten minutes just to wind down. Allow your mind to wander. Daydream. Reflect back on a happy memory. Consider the ways God has blessed you over the past week and express gratitude to Him. Don't fall into a legalistic trap in which you feel like solitude *always* has to be devoted to prayer and spiritual growth. The type of solitude I'm advocating in this chapter takes place apart from the time you spend in God's Word and in prayer.

Try this exercise for five days straight without fail. Prioritize it like you would treat brushing your teeth or checking in on your kids. Make this time nonnegotiable, even if you're not sure you can spare the time. Now that you've gone through the intervention in

Part One and have begun to purge some unnecessary things from your life, you should have some extra time for solitude (or at least have a plan in place to make it happen). You deserve it.

Embracing the Quiet

When my generation was growing up, boredom was a standard rite of passage. If you wanted to spend time with a friend, you had two choices: (1) walk to her house and knock on the door, or (2) call her home phone and hope her mom wasn't engaged in a marathon chat session with her best friend. If you wanted to watch a TV show, you had five channels from which to choose. And stations didn't offer many kid-friendly programs, so unless you turned it on to *The Brady Bunch* or *Gilligan's Island*, you were out of luck. Video games didn't become an option until my late high school years. Even so, there was only so much Atari *Pong* you could play before the monotony of moving a paddle up and down on a screen grew old. Really old. We had fewer choices and fewer activities bidding for our attention, so it wasn't uncommon to find ourselves with nothing to do, which was actually a good thing. We had to find ways to entertain ourselves. We embraced quiet and solitude and learned how to breathe while in those gaps between schoolwork and recreation. And we were richer for it.

How ironic that so many of us who grew up in a generation that provided ample opportunities for solitude have forgotten its benefits in our adult years. Even more troubling, we have robbed our children of the benefits of solitude by filling their lives with too much activity and stimuli. Their only hope of experiencing any version of quiet takes place when we send them to time-out or when they go to sleep at night. We as parents have conditioned our children to view boredom as a bad thing. In fact, when my kids were young and whined about being bored, I had a list of chores ready to go. "You're bored? Here's a damp cloth. Now, go wipe down the baseboards." Yes, putting my bored little urchins to work saved me a little housework, but I wonder if a better approach would have been to tell them, "Good! You're supposed to be bored every now and then. Believe me, when you're older, you will crave boredom. Enjoy it while you can." If I could go back and do it over again, I'd teach my kids that boredom is not a bad thing and model to them the benefits of solitude. I would think up a list of creative ways to help them not only engage in solitude but enjoy it.

Here are a few ideas you might try with your children if they struggle with boredom and solitude:

- Lay out a blanket on the front lawn, set the timer, and tell them to enjoy God's beautiful creation.
- Tell them to close their eyes for five minutes and pretend they are in one of their favorite places. At the end of the five minutes, have them share what they imagined.
- The next time it rains, tell them to sit on your covered porch and watch the rain in silence.
- Consider establishing a set amount of quiet time each day to devote to solitary activities.
- Look over the list of "100 Ways to Give It a Rest" on pages 193–202 for more ideas.

The quiet gaps my generation experienced are all but extinct among today's kids. Limitless distractions bombard this group of kids, keeping them entertained around the clock. With social media, the Internet, and smartphones, the party never ends. Rather than draw necessary boundaries in an effort to teach our children the benefits of solitude, many of us compound the problem even more by filling their days with extracurricular activities and, thus, reinforcing the message that idle time is wasted time. One can only wonder what long-term effects this generation will experience because anyone can opt out of solitude by turning to any number of escapes, from movies on demand to videos on one's phone. Children (and adults) need time for uninterrupted introspection free from the self-consciousness they often experience while in the presence of others. In solitude we come face-to-face with our true selves, and our identities are formed. Most importantly, solitude allows children (and adults) to know and hear from God.

When I was a little girl, I would lie on my sloped driveway by myself on warm summer nights and watch the stars above me. Such solitude didn't seem weird or awkward at the time but, rather, something children were *supposed to* do. Never mind that those times of quiet also left me thoroughly convinced that God lived on the moon. I wasn't raised in the church, but I had been told that God lived in the heavens and was watching over us. So I logically concluded He lived on the moon. Obviously the sun was far too hot (only a few degrees warmer than a summer afternoon in Texas), so where else could God live? Besides, when I lay on the driveway, looking up into the sky, I could see His silhouette in the shadowy portion of the moon in the bottom left quadrant. It looked as if God were curled up, sleeping peacefully in His lunar condo. And that is what convinced me that God lived in the moon—until my theory was dashed one day in science class. My teacher explained that the shadowy part of the moon was caused by hot lava that poured out on the moon's surface many years ago and appears darker than the rest of the surface because that dried lava doesn't reflect the sunlight.

My theology might have been a bit off, but in those quiet gaps when I would lie pondering on my driveway under the starry heavens, my heart was first stirred with thoughts of God. I am deeply concerned about the generations coming behind me who have been taught to fear quiet lulls of boredom and rush to fill them with meaningless white noise. I have felt the pull myself and constantly have had to remind myself of the benefits of solitude. None of us stands a chance of developing or retaining an inward solitude unless we recognize its importance and fight for it. Apart from this aloneness, we cannot know God.

But that's not all. Without solitude, we cannot discover the person God wants us to be. Only when our hearts are still and receptive can He unlock the mysteries of how He created us and then mold our identities according to His life-changing gospel of grace. Solitude allows us the time needed to marinate in His truths and define our identity according to who we are in Christ. Without solitude, we will strive and rush to conform to the world's preferences. No wonder our souls lack rest.

Shushing Our Souls

While I was visiting with my literary agent on the phone recently, he shared that he had just returned from a silent retreat where he went camping alone for several days. Other than a few bare essentials (food, clothing, and shelter) tucked in a backpack, all he took was a blank journal and a pen. No cell phone. No laptop. No radio. No books. He didn't even take his Bible because he wanted to ensure he was still before God in a listening posture. Other than a handful of people he saw hiking the trails by day, he was essentially alone. Alone with his thoughts. Alone with his dreams. Alone with reminders of God's handiwork. Alone with his Maker and absolutely no interruptions to distract him from hearing God's still, quiet voice. I suppose he wasn't really *alone*.

As he shared his experience, his excitement was contagious. By the time we hung up, I was ready to give this silent retreat thing a try. Well, except for the part about sleeping in a tent. In the woods. And having no phone. Or indoor plumbing. Or electrical outlet to plug in my hair dryer. Or a wagon big enough to haul all my Trader Joe's snacks. Aside from the fact that I have zero survival skills, I also happen to be a huge scaredy-cat, and last I checked, wild animals and serial killers live in the woods. So, yeah, now that I think about it, you can count me out on a silent retreat if camping in the woods is required. If I were to embark on a silent retreat for the purpose of catching my breath, camping would not make it on my list of relaxation-friendly accommodations.

Even if I substituted the tent in the deep woods with a penthouse in a luxury five-star hotel, I have to wonder: *Could I thrive (or even survive) a weekend with just a pen, a notebook, God, and me?* (I'm guessing those of you who have little ones or even teens are more than happy to give it a try—even if it's a Motel 6.) On the one hand, the thought of taking a silent retreat for the purpose of disconnecting from the world and reconnecting with God sounds so enticing. But on the other hand, I have some serious hesitations about *that much* solitude. Would I run out of things to say? (I suppose that's the point.) Would I cave in and turn on the TV? Especially if my retreat overlapped with the season finale of *Dancing with the Stars*? Would I make a midnight run to the nearest drugstore for contraband like the latest edition of *Southern Living* magazine and a disposable cell phone? Would I raid the vending machines to engage in a three-day comfort-eating binge?

Probably yes to all of the above. All of which indicate I am more at home in the world than I am with God. That hurts my heart just to read that last sentence. I've often said, "Jesus is my *everything*," so why then would it be such a struggle if He were to be my *only thing* for just a few days?

Room for Improvement

Henri Nouwen called solitude "the furnace of transformation." He went on to say,

> In solitude I get rid of my scaffolding: no friends to talk with, no telephone calls to make, no meetings to attend, no music to entertain, no books to distract, just me—naked, vulnerable, weak, sinful, deprived, broken—nothing. It is this nothingness that I have to face in my solitude, a nothingness so dreadful that everything in me wants to run to my friends, my work, and my distractions so that I can forget my nothingness and make myself believe that I am worth something.[8]

In prolonged periods of solitude, God speaks to our hearts about where we find our worth and prompts us to "cease striving" (Ps. 46:10 NASB). Solitude provides a safe place to ask big questions and ponder an even bigger God. It is the space in which we can plumb the depths of our souls and learn to examine our hearts. Like the psalmist, we are called to invite God to search our hearts and render a verdict.

Search me, O God, and know my heart!
Try me and know my thoughts!

And see if there be any grievous way in me,
and lead me in the way everlasting! (Ps. 139:23–24)

The idea of inviting God to search our hearts can be a bit unsettling. We must remember God's purpose in examining our hearts. Hearts cannot be thoroughly examined while juggling a steady stream of interruptions and distractions. It's just not possible. Many Christians stay busy and avoid solitude because they fear what God will show them regarding their motives and affections.

In his book *Intimacy with the Almighty*, author and pastor Charles Swindoll said:

> An inner restlessness grows within us when we refuse to get alone and examine our own hearts, including our motives. As our lives begin to pick up the debris that accompanies a lot of activities and involvements, we can train ourselves to go right on, to stay active, to be busy in the Lord's work. Unless we discipline ourselves to pull back, to get alone for the hard work of self-examination in times of solitude, serenity will remain only a distant dream. How busy we can become . . . and as a result, how empty! We mouth words, but they mean nothing. We find ourselves trafficking in unlived truths. We fake spirituality.[9]

Solitude allows us the space and time to bare our hearts and souls before a holy God and to ask Him to reveal areas of our lives that need improvement. Where else would this examination take place if not in solitude? Ralph Waldo Emerson is quoted as having once said, "God enters by a private door into every individual."[10] We can't put deadbolts on the doors of our hearts. Only those who *want* to be refined will allow God to purge away the impurities that lie deep within. When we understand that God judges our motives and affections as an act of His unfailing love for us (and not anger or spite), and when we keep that love ever before us, only then can we walk continually in His truth. But first, we must be willing to be still and listen.

REST STOP

1. What is your biggest hindrance to solitude? Do you view solitude as an essential discipline or an optional activity? (Answer the question based on your behavior rather than knowledge of what is right.)

2. When did you last go "away by yourself to a secluded place to rest awhile"? Describe the time and, more importantly, how it impacted your soul.

3. If you have children, what steps are you taking to teach them the benefits of solitude? Better yet, how are you modeling it as a discipline in your own life?

4. Think of a time when God used solitude to refine or transform your soul. How might that situation have been different if you had not taken time to be alone with Him?

The One-Week Dare

This challenge is a double dare. First, I dare you to set aside fifteen to thirty minutes each day over the next week to spend some time in solitude. If necessary, set an alarm to remind you. Remember, this time does not replace your Bible study or prayer time, nor is it meant to be leisure time. The main goal is to "come away" and catch your breath for the sake of restoring your soul. Whether you decide to retreat to your "quiet zone" or find a quiet spot somewhere nearby, the space does not matter as long as it is conducive to solitude.

Now for the hard part. I dare you to fast from all social media and nonessential technology (aside from work-related and/or family obligations) during this one-week period. Stay off Facebook, Instagram, Twitter, and Pinterest completely. I promise you can do it. Close your laptop. Turn off the TV. Put away your tablet. Tell your friends and close family members to contact your spouse, or other designated person, in case of an emergency. If it is not possible to completely fast from technology, choose one device and use it for emergencies only, such as urgent texts to and from your children.

The purpose of this exercise is threefold: First, by pulling away for a week, it will give you more free time to engage in solitude unencumbered and without distractions. No dings, chimes, buzzes, chirps, scrolling newsfeeds, or other needless stimuli to rob your soul of peace. Second, it will serve as an exercise to prove that you are not mastered by your devices. (Remember, they should answer to you, rather than the other way around.) Finally by the end of the week, the exercise should give you a basic awareness of how an overly tethered life can rob your soul of much-needed solitude and soul rest. And whet your appetite to make some necessary adjustments.

Bonus: For extra credit, I dare you to plan a mini silent retreat to take place sometime during the next thirty to sixty days. For most people, taking off for several days would take significant planning, but you can likely square away twenty-four to thirty-six hours. The most important factor is choosing a solitary and quiet place with no interruptions (e.g., leave your phone behind or turn it off; abstain from all media). If you must take your phone or can't bear the thought of being disconnected the entire time, consider turning it on only twice a day to check for any important messages. Keep your retreat as simple as possible. Take only a few essentials. If you want to take your Bible, that is fine, but also allow plenty of time to listen to God, pray, think about your life, and dream about the future.

7

Give Yourself a Break

Time for Leisure

I stared at the form for five minutes before I could think of an answer. My publisher requested an updated bio, and I had gotten hung up on the last question: "What do you do for leisure?" Crickets chirped in the background. No answer. Not even a thought. The word *leisure* was tripping me up, so I looked it up in my online dictionary just to make sure I had a full understanding of the word. Here's the definition I found: "*time* or *opportunity* for ease, relaxation."[1] More crickets. Followed by a healthy dose of conviction. So *that's* the problem. Thanks to my unhappy habit of filling every gap in my day with some form of work-related activity, I had no margin to do something I actually enjoy.

I pondered the question on the bio for a bit longer and finally settled on saying, "When my schedule allows, I enjoy spending time with my family and perusing antique and thrift stores and yard sales for vintage finds." While I do enjoy both my family and shopping for vintage finds, my choice of wording revealed my warped perspective with regard to leisure. "When my schedule allows . . ." Have you ever said that? Stated this way, the answer shows the true approach to the way we spend our days—at the mercy of a calendar. However, our schedules shouldn't manage us—we should manage our schedules. Until we understand the importance and value of leisure, it will continue to be an afterthought, something we plan to get around to "someday."

Since filling out that bio form, I have made great strides in making leisure a consistent part of my life, but doing so required an entire attitude adjustment. Admitting leisure was necessary for the well-being of my soul was only the first step in reordering my priorities. The hardest part was ridding my daily schedule of other things in order to have opportunities and time for leisure. (Much of what I eliminated were enemies of rest and needed to be eliminated anyway.) Old habits die hard, and I still find myself tempted to lapse back into a pace of chronic busyness. However, after reaping the benefit of a more-rested soul, I am determined to stay the course of leisure.

Leisure is much more than an occasional Sunday-afternoon nap or a coffee date with a friend. It helps bring balance to your life and rest to your soul. Leisure allows you to catch your breath in the race before the next heat begins. Reread that last sentence and take a minute to reflect on that truth. Do you believe it? Maybe your race involves a full-time job or a long week of caring for the needs of your family. Or maybe your race involves juggling both. You need something (leisure) to look forward to, or you will burn out.

Unfortunately many of us are running our races as sprints rather than as marathons. We run hard and fast so that someday we'll arrive at the finish line and earn the prize of leisure. The problem is the finish line keeps moving, and we never experience the joys of leisure. Long-distance runners know the key to running is to take it one leg at a time and run at a steady pace. They have learned to tune out the other runners who blaze past them in the surrounding lanes. They will see those runners again—when those runners are heaving their chests and gasping for breath. Leisure slows the pace and allows us to see our days one leg at a time.

How are you running the race? Have you factored in the stops along the way? Or have you postponed leisure as something you plan to get around to when you cross the finish line someday? Deferred leisure never happens because it is pinned on a hope rather than practiced as a reality. Leisure was intended to be a reward for your hard work on this earth while you live on this earth. It's okay to give work (volunteer or otherwise) a rest. Quit waiting for *someday* to enjoy a hobby or activity. Someday will never arrive unless you decide to graft it into your ongoing routine.

Just for Fun

How would you answer this question: "What do you do for leisure?"

Do you spend the bulk of your time engaged in your children's extracurricular lives? Do you get together with friends on the weekends? Do you have a favorite hobby? Do you exercise? Go on dates with your husband? There are no hard-and-fast rules about leisure, except that it provides opportunity for ease and relaxation.

What one person might put in the leisure column, another might file in the work column. For example, some people find great enjoyment in cooking. They can't *wait* to get in the kitchen to experiment with new recipes and try them out on their family and friends. (P.S., If this describes you, I'd like to be on your list of friends.)

However, others (ahem, me, *cough, cough*) would consider cooking a chore or a necessary evil, especially if it involves anything beyond microwave-heating instructions. Or take shopping, for example. I have heard rumors that some women hate to shop for new clothes (or even shoes!). I was hesitant to believe the rumors until I met my mother-in-law. Her wardrobe would have to disintegrate in the dryer before she would engage in a shopping spree. She loathes shopping as much as I loathe cooking.

The Bible is full of examples of leisure activities ranging from eating, drinking, dancing, music, gardening, star gazing, and more. In fact, if you are looking for biblical support to sleep in on occasion, Psalm 127:2 advises, "It is in vain that you rise up early and go late to rest, eating the bread of anxious toil; for he gives to his beloved sleep." You're welcome for that one. King Solomon concluded, "I perceived that there is nothing better for them than to be joyful and to do good as long as they live; also that everyone should eat and drink and take pleasure in all his toil—this is God's gift to man" (Eccl. 3:12–13). Leisure is a gift to be enjoyed. Given the Bible's endorsement of leisure, why, then, is it such a struggle for many of us to enjoy it?

Granted, leisure looks much different today. According to a 2013 survey by the Bureau of Labor Statistics, Americans spent an average of 5.1 hours of leisure (defined as nonworking hours) per day. Sadly, more than half of those available hours were spent watching TV (2.8 hours). "Socializing and communicating" garnered an average of thirty-nine minutes, and "playing games; using computer for leisure" represented twenty-five minutes. Trailing at the end of the list of leisure activities in last place was a mere seventeen minutes devoted to "relaxing and thinking."[2] I can't help but notice that the majority of our leisure has involved engaging with media or technology that, in large doses, has been proven to take a greater toll on our souls.

In Ephesians 5, Paul warned, "Be very careful, then, how you live—not as unwise but as wise, making the most of every opportunity, because the days are evil" (vv. 15–16 NIV). If the ultimate purpose of leisure is to provide rest and relaxation, we need to be careful that we don't choose leisure activities that are counterproductive to that purpose. For many of us, the real problem is not a lack of *time* to devote to leisure, but rather a devotion to the wrong *kinds* of leisure.

Empty Leisure

You're tired. I get that. It's been a long day. You arrived at work only to receive a frantic call from your daughter saying she forgot her English paper at home and will get a zero if she doesn't have it to turn in by fifth period. You spend your lunch hour fetching the English paper and dropping it off at the school. By the time you leave the office at the end of the day, you still have e-mails to answer later that evening. For now, you race to the ball field to catch your son's baseball game. You meet your family at the park and head to the concession stand for a nutritious dinner of hot dogs, nachos, and popcorn. After the game, you drive home and begin the homework showdown. You pack lunches, fold some laundry, sign necessary forms, and reply to the work e-mails that went unanswered.

If you are a stay-at-home mom, maybe this sounds familiar. You woke up at five thirty when your little one wanted to tell you about a bad dream he had. You would like to go back to sleep, but your grade-school-aged child needs breakfast and a lunch packed, and it's off to the races. Your day is spent making cupcakes for the school party, running errands, and taking your little guy to the park because he's logged too much time on your tablet already. While at the park you tap a grocery list into your phone, and then you head to the store to replenish the pantry, all before school lets out and it's time to pick up your oldest. Then it's homework, soccer practice, dinnertime, laundry, and that extra story your toddler begged you to read at bedtime.

Finally, you have a spare moment—twenty minutes to be exact—before you crawl into your bed and collapse. You do what comes naturally—turn on the TV and begin to surf through the channels, catching bits and pieces of shows. Or maybe you log onto Facebook to scan your newsfeed. Oh sure, these activities feel relaxing at first, especially when you watch the heartwarming video clip of the latest marriage proposal to go viral. Your laughter is short-lived, however. Back on your newsfeed, you click on an article about school bullying and briefly consider homeschooling your children. After reading the bullying article, you hop over to a friend's profile to take a peek at the vacation album she just posted. Wait, is that what she *really* looks like in a swimsuit? Seriously, does she work out every day to look that good? You put down the sleeve of Ritz crackers you were munching on and sigh heavily. By the time you log off forty-five minutes later (you had to finish reading the article on the evils of gluten), you feel anything but relaxed. That is the problem with counterfeit leisure. It's like junk food to your soul. It steals your time but leaves nothing of value in return.

Nothing is wrong with engaging in social media or other forms of media in our leisure time, but we need to pay careful attention to how the activity makes us feel in the process. If surfing social media reaches a point where it becomes counterproductive, we need to exercise self-control and disengage. Leisure should be life-giving, not soul-draining. One wise question to ask before engaging in any form of leisure would be, "Is _____ [name the activity] good for my soul?" This includes our standard go-to leisure outlets that we unconsciously indulge in with little thought given to the consequences.

In addition to being more aware of counterfeit leisure, we also need to be mindful of unholy leisure. Ephesians 5:11 warns, "And have no fellowship with the unfruitful works of darkness, but rather reprove them" (KJV). One Bible commentary says, "The point of this exhortation is in the adjective 'unfruitful.' The works of darkness are unfruitful; they produce no goodness, give rise to no satisfaction, to no moral results that are 'a joy forever;' or, if fruit they have, it is shame, remorse, despair."[3] Most of us probably think of the really big, obvious sins when we read the phrase "unfruitful works of darkness," but plenty of leisure activities fall into a gray area. Perhaps our decisions should be based on whether the activities are fruitful.

The next time you engage in a leisure activity, do a soul check when your time ends. If it didn't leave you feeling more at ease and relaxed (the definition of leisure), it's not really leisure. In fact, it becomes just one more thing that weighs heavily on your soul.

Off the Clock

"Hi, honey, I'm home." When my generation was growing up, the dividing line between work and play was clear in the majority of

American families. Dad walked through the door after a long day at work, plopped down his briefcase in the foyer, kissed his wife on the cheek as she tended to something on the stovetop, and just like that, the workday officially ended and leisure time began. Most of the time that briefcase stayed in the foyer, untouched until the next morning when the workday began again. The evening hours were sacred. Employers and coworkers didn't dare call you at home unless it was an emergency.

Today it is nearly impossible to leave our work at work. Whether you have a full-time job outside the home or stay home with your children, chances are you have a hard time clocking out. If you are a mother, your workday bleeds over into the evening hours, regardless of whether you work in or outside the home. Once you factor in dinnertime preparation, homework, extracurricular activities, and the bedtime drill, you are lucky if you can grab a spare minute to catch your breath before your head hits the pillow and you wake up and start the routine all over again.

The term *work* is nebulous, so it's hard to clock out officially and leave work behind. We may leave one kind of work in the office only to pick up a different kind of work at home. This is one reason so many of us experience unrest in our souls. In addition, technology has made us accessible around the clock, and many employers assume that employees will be available to discuss or solve work problems into the evening hours. It's no wonder we never quite feel rested. Even if we don't have paid full-time jobs, we likely have felt the after-hours pull to answer e-mails, texts, or Facebook messages related to volunteer or social activities. This typically flies under the radar and fails to get labeled as "work," but if it prohibits us from catching our breaths and relaxing, it is work. By not setting aside a clear block of time to devote to leisure rest, we end up grazing on tiny nibbles of sporadic, mind-numbing activities and wonder why we never seem to feel rested.

One study found that employees in the UK with smartphones worked an extra two hours each day.[4] Full-time just became overtime, but rarely are employees paid for work outside of the standard workday. In another study German researchers examined the effects of employees taking their work home with them in the evenings or on the weekends. The researchers found "that the workers were plagued by a host of issues, including cardiovascular problems, insomnia, headaches, muscular issues, fatigue, anxiety, and stomach problems." Lead author Dr. Anna Arlinghaus said, "Our findings indicate that even a small amount of supplemental work beyond contractually agreed work hours can lead to health issues. The correlation is very strong." The authors concluded, "Free time should be free time, otherwise it must be expected that it cannot fulfill functions of recovery and recuperation."[5]

One German carmaker, Daimler, decided to become proactive in helping its employees protect their vacation time. The company installed software on its employees' computers that deletes e-mails if the workers are on vacation. Daimler hires more than 100,000 employees, and company spokesman Oliver Wihofszki explained, "The idea behind it is to give people a break and let them rest. Then they can come back to work with a fresh spirit."[6]

A Much-Needed Sabbatical

The idea that laborers need time to break away and refresh their spirits is not a new concept. It can be traced back to the beginning of time, when God modeled the principle of Sabbath rest so that we could enjoy the fruit of our hard work. While many of us are familiar with the biblical model of Sabbath rest, many of us are unfamiliar with another rest—a sabbatical year. In Exodus, God told the Israelites, "For six years you shall sow your land and gather in its yield, but the seventh year you shall let it rest and lie fallow, that the poor of your people may eat; and what they leave the beasts of the field may eat. You shall do likewise with your vineyard, and with your olive orchard" (Ex. 23:10–11).

Even today many Israeli farmers still practice the sabbatical year. They allow the fields and orchards to lie fallow for the entire year. Among the rules of one community in Haifa, Israel, are: "Don't plant crops, don't lay new grass, just take care of what exists, and don't add anything new." The sabbatical or, as it's called, the *Shmita*, means more than just allowing the land to rest. One farmer living near Tiberias in the northern Galilee region said, "As religious Jews, during the year, we learn more Torah, we free our farmers to learn more about our faith. Our religion says: leave work and work on your spirit."[7]

Compare this practice to the 40 percent of American workers, according to another study, who can't seem to bring themselves to break away from their jobs to exercise their paid vacation days accumulated during the year. The reasons were especially revealing. At the top of the list was "the dread of returning from a vacation to piles of work (40 percent)." This excuse was followed by "the belief that no one will be able to step in and do their job for them while they're gone (35 percent), not being able to afford it (33 percent) and the fear of being seen as replaceable (22 percent). 'Americans suffer from a work martyr complex,' said Roger Dow, president and CEO of the U.S. Travel Association. 'In part, it's because "busyness" is something we wear as a badge of honor.'"[8]

The Israeli farmers leave their work behind for one year to

"work on their spirit," but we can't even take a few paid-vacation days to work on ours. No wonder we're so exhausted. If we are to gain rest for our souls, we must be vigilant in setting aside leisure time and establishing firm boundaries to protect it. Let me also suggest that taking a rest from work should include our volunteer activities. In fact, it wouldn't be a bad idea to take a break from ministry activities every seven years, especially if we serve in full-time ministry at any level.

One women's ministry director shared that she was about to take a much-needed sabbatical from her duties for two months. The church had had a couple of staff members leave the year prior, and she was carrying an unbearable load in their absence while the church searched for people to fill the positions. She shared that she was nearing the point of extreme burnout, and the sabbatical would allow her to catch her breath and return refreshed and ready to serve again. She knew she had to leave work behind to allow God to work on her spirit. Even though she had set firm boundaries and sent out a notice to her coworkers and ministry team members to remind them she would be unavailable (even via e-mail), one person replied and asked if she would be attending the elder's meeting the following week. This story is a reminder that even when we attempt to establish a clear division between our work and leisure rest, some people will still expect us to be on the clock. Be aware of these land mines, and be prepared to defuse them.

A New, Rested You

A friend of mine (fellow author/speaker) vigilantly blocks out every Monday as a day for solitude and rest. Her husband is a pastor, so Sundays are workdays for both of them. Monday is her day to rest and recharge after a busy week and weekend. She moves at an unhurried pace and enjoys the things that minister to her soul. She might read a book, take a bubble bath, work in her garden, or bake some homemade bread, depending on her mood that day. Sometimes she doesn't even get out of her pj's. When she first told me about her "do-nothing day," I initially judged her. However, I quickly realized that my judgmental attitude stemmed from a place of envy and jealousy because she didn't feel a shred of guilt over devoting an entire day to rest.

I feel guilty thumbing through a magazine or engaging in an occasional fiction read. Even when I slow down, my mind still races, haunted by a never-ending to-do list and a sea of deadlines. Somewhere along the way, I bought into the lie that having idle time is a sign of laziness. I was taught in church (early in my journey) that good Christians should always be busy doing kingdom work. Always. Every empty block of time should be devoted to church work, soul-winning, or combating social injustice. Who has time to take a bubble bath when so many people are dying of starvation? Living without water? Being victimized by sex trafficking? And we wonder why so many believers are exhausted and burned-out on religion. We claim to rest in grace, but we are swept up in the current of works-based religion. Our calendars and constant weariness expose our inner struggles. God Himself rested on the seventh day and modeled the concept of taking a Sabbath rest, yet so many of us can't seem to follow His lead without feeling guilt and anxiety.

Many of us, unfortunately, have branded "me time" as a form of laziness. We have heard sermons on Proverbs 6, which contrasts the sluggard to the busy ant, and we believe there is no middle ground. We are either the lazy sluggard or the busy ant. Women are encouraged to emulate the esteemed Proverbs 31 woman (who, for the record, was not a real woman, but rather a list of ideal qualities that make up a virtuous woman). We are taught that she "does not eat the bread of idleness" (v. 27). We believe this includes any activity that is not dedicated to God and/or family. Forget about indulging in an HGTV *House Hunters* marathon. Idleness! Off to get a mani/pedi? Idleness! Thumbing through a copy of *Southern Living*? Idleness! (Unless you are looking for new recipes to make for your family, then it's only partial idleness, right?) Reading a novel? Idleness! (Deduct more points if it's not a Christian novel.)

If we take a closer look at Proverbs 31:27, the verse that discourages idleness, we would discover that the preceding phrase states, "She looks well to the ways of her household." This verse speaks to an imbalance when "eat[ing] the bread of idleness" takes priority over "look[ing] well to the ways of her household." The Hebrew word for "eat" is *âkal*, and it means to "burn up, consume, or devour."[9] This brand of idleness dismisses hard work and is rooted in selfishness. This verse was a warning against the kind of idleness spoken of in 2 Thessalonians 3:11, where Paul wrote, "For we hear that some among you walk in idleness, not busy at work, but busybodies." The NASB translation uses the phrase "leading an undisciplined life" rather than "walk in idleness." Interestingly, two verses later, Paul also warns, "As for you, brothers, do not grow weary in doing good" (v. 13).

One of the best ways to guard against growing "weary in doing good" is to schedule soul-enriching time throughout the week. Most people can't set aside an entire day each week, but they can set aside moments throughout the week. If you work full-time during the day, and you've been carrying the bulk of the load in the evenings to take care of your family, you should delegate some of the tasks to your husband. If you are a single mother, consider trading childcare with a friend or asking a family member to watch the kids so you can take a break and pamper yourself on occasion. Regardless, make it happen.

Let me address this issue in another way: "What do you do for *you*?" Does the thought of caring for yourself make you uneasy? Why? Do you feel guilty if your time is not devoted to some utilitarian purpose or the enrichment of others? I know how you feel. I've been there. A lot. However, I want you to think about something: If you do not give yourself a break, your family will suffer. (Not to mention, you will teach your children the same unhealthy pattern.) If you fill every waking moment with productivity, your productivity will take a hit. God intended for you to have margin in your life for refreshing your spirit and recharging your batteries. Doing things you enjoy—whether bowling or backgammon— enriches your life and makes you more able to engage fully in the tasks you face.

Some of you have never taken time to do something for yourself, so trying it out might seem scary or overwhelming. You may have never had permission to nurture yourself, so I'm giving you permission now. Here are a few ways you can take care of yourself in case you don't know where to start:

- Take a bubble bath with a strict "do not interrupt Mommy" rule.
- Schedule a mani/pedi after work one day.
- If you have little ones, rotate the bedtime ritual with your husband. Read a book or watch a favorite TV show on your night off.
- Read a biography of someone you admire. Check out the

latest mystery thriller. Explore the history of your state. Just choose something that piques your interest.

- Take a walk, even if it's just to the end of your block and back.
- Go to a bookstore and peruse the books just for fun. You can even buy one.
- Consider investing in a porch swing. If you don't have a porch, hang a swing from a tree or find a self-standing swing. Make it your getaway spot.
- Cultivate a flowerbed.
- Make yourself a cup of hot tea. (Even better, enjoy it on your swing with a good book.)
- Splurge and get a massage.
- Browse around a new store that you've been meaning to visit. (Unless this leaves you feeling dissatisfied over what you don't have. In that case, stay away.)
- Play a game on your computer, tablet, or phone (Solitaire, Words with Friends, Sudoku, and so forth).
- Create an online photo book. It's easy to find coupons to get them at a good price because of the competitive market.
- Devote some time to a new hobby you've always wanted to take up. Try needlepoint, knitting, learning a new language, making jewelry, chalk painting, calligraphy, or skydiving. The sky is the limit, no pun intended.

One hobby I've always wanted to pursue is pressing flowers. A few months ago I found a microwaveable flower press kit online and told my husband I wanted it for Valentine's Day. Forget the candy and live flowers. On second thought, give me the kit *and* the flowers, and I'll preserve them forever. Unfortunately the flower press kit sat unopened for a month while I scrambled to make a book deadline. Finally one day I decided to put down my work and open my present. I was suffering from a brief spell of writer's block and pulled the kit out and read the directions. I had just picked some wildflowers the day before while out on a short walk. I put them in between the plastic trays and zapped them in the microwave for fifteen seconds as instructed.

I was amazed at how beautiful the flowers looked, but even more amazed at how I felt after my short leisure break. When I went back to my writing, I felt a new surge of energy, and my writer's block lifted. The short leisure break actually made my work *more* productive. The next week I continued the project by painting a couple of wooden picture frames I had picked up from a thrift store for fifty cents (another favorite hobby of mine). I put a quick coat of chalk paint on each frame, distressed them lightly with a piece of sandpaper, and, voilà, I had new frames for my newly pressed wildflowers. Today they hang on my wall, and seeing them brings me joy because *I* created that artwork. My total time investment was about one hour over a two-week period. That small investment yielded a huge payoff to my soul.

We rationalize that when our work, commitments, and deadlines bear down on us, we must abandon leisure for increased output. It seems counterproductive to take a short break to do something we enjoy, but in the end, that leisure results in an unexpected outcome. We are *most* productive when we can look forward to something, even if it's a short break to recharge our souls.

You work hard, and you deserve to give yourself a break. What brings you joy and takes your mind off the pressures of commitments and work? Find a way to do more of it. Your soul will thank you.

Wanna Get Away?

Many of us remember as kids counting down the days until Christmas break, spring break, and, most of all, summer break. Those breaks gave us something to look forward to during the year and helped break up the monotony of the school routine. When we enter the grown-up world, we don't outgrow the need for an extended break. We need a planned interruption to break up the monotony of our daily routines. This is true whether we work outside the home or stay at home with our kids. We need a vacation. While I doubt our employers (or our spouses) would approve of our taking the entire summer off, we need to get away for a few days or more and decompress. In fact, vacations are good for our overall health. According to WebMD, people who take vacations experience lower stress, less risk of heart disease, a better outlook on life, and more motivation to achieve goals. The report goes on to say, "The biggest boost in happiness comes from planning the vacation. You can feel the effects up to 8 weeks before your trip. And when you're done with that retreat, start planning the next one. Simply having something to look forward to can be rewarding."[10]

I am blessed that I married a man who grew up taking a family vacation every year, without fail. For that reason, he was committed to carrying on the tradition. Our vacations are living proof that a big budget isn't necessary to go on a family trip. Some of our family's greatest get-away memories are the budget-friendly trips we took to nearby state parks and rented cabins. We packed lunches each day and found scenic picnic spots to enjoy them. We fished, skimmed rocks, hiked, and played board games at night. My husband even involved our kids in the trip-planning process on the front end, which helped build excitement in the days leading up to the vacation. One year we went to Arkansas, and he let each one of our kids pick an activity to do on their assigned day (horseback riding, hiking, a wildlife park, and so on). Honestly, our kids talk more about that trip than the one we later took to Disney World.

If you are married, I highly recommend that you get away as a couple every once in a while, even if it means alternating one year for family vacation and the next year for a couple's vacation. (You can send the kids to their grandparents' house for some fun.) Even if you can only spare time for a weekend getaway, that time nurtures your marriage and models to your children that your marriage is a priority. Your destination does not need to be exotic. Even a short drive to a nearby town for a couple of nights gives you something to look forward to during the year and offers a reprieve from the monotony of work and the challenges that come with raising children. Ideally, you want to factor in a longer vacation (one week or more) once every three to five years. Couples who play together, stay together.

One note of caution when planning a vacation, whether it is with your husband or your family: resist the temptation to schedule so many activities each day that you defeat the purpose of a vacation. My husband is a trip-planner extraordinaire who likes to get the biggest bang for his buck and maximize every spare moment with nonstop sight-seeing activities. In the early years, I often felt like I needed a vacation to recover from the vacation. Can I get a witness? We had to have a little come-to-Jesus meeting over the trip itinerary, and I am happy to say he has come a long way over the years. We now try to schedule a day or two when we have no schedule—no planned activities, no places to visit or monuments to see. We can sit around and take it slow or do absolutely nothing.

When it comes to rest, we need to remember that *doing nothing* is actually *doing something*, especially if inactivity allows us time to catch our breaths and invigorate our souls.

If your budget won't allow for a family or a couple's vacation in the near future, consider taking a staycation, where you take off time from work and take advantage of local attractions in your community. The important thing is that you take a break from the demands of everyday life. You might even consider planning a trip a year or more in advance and setting aside money as you earn it to go toward the trip. If it's a family vacation, involve the kids in the process and help them think of ways to earn money for the vacation fund (lemonade stand, garage sale, and so forth). Put pictures on your refrigerator of things you want to do on the trip, and keep the collection jar/box visible so you all can measure the progress along the way. It gives your kids some ownership of the trip and bonds the family together in the process.

Playing for Keeps

If you struggle with allowing your work to bleed into your leisure time, I encourage you to set some firm boundaries. Only you can solve the problem of overwork. The daily demands of your job will hijack your leisure time until you decide to take some drastic measures to protect it. Personally, I have been extremely convicted over the amount of work I do in the evenings and have been taking steps to "clock out" and take back my personal time, but it hasn't been easy.

Here are a few disciplines I have cultivated in an effort to create the essential separation. And remember, if you stay home full-time with your children, you are working.

1. I shut down my laptop or desk computer when my husband walks in the door at the end of the day. I get online one last time to check e-mail and tie up any loose ends by 7:30 p.m. After that time, I try not to reopen e-mail until the following morning. Your schedule will dictate when you can shut down. The important thing is to set a time when your workday is officially over. If you don't establish a formal ending time, your work will stay with you the entire evening, even flittering through your mind and distracting you from your family. If you want to get on your computer for leisure purposes, log out of your e-mail so you're not tempted to hop over and check it. You might also try to limit the number of times you check e-mail on the weekends. (I allow myself two times to check e-mail on Saturday and try to abstain completely from checking it on Sunday.)

2. Some employers have begun texting their employees after standard business hours, so it might be necessary to establish some boundaries in that area as well. Your supervisor will quickly get the message if you send a reply text the next morning saying, "I just got this message. Sorry, but I don't check work-related texts when I'm off work in order to protect my family time." Few can argue with that (though some might).

3. Turn off all notification alerts on your cell phone, and try not to check e-mail on your phone or other devices. Managing your time presents its own challenges, and adding other apps, dings, whistles, and alerts that vie for your time only counters your efforts. Tell your close

family members and friends that they can call you if they are unable to reach you by e-mail or text.

These practical steps won't work for everyone, and I am not trying to be legalistic. However, I am challenging you to take proactive measures for the sake of restoring your soul. Come up with a plan that works for you and helps you take back your leisure time. Your soul's vitality hangs in the balance.

Whether you are long overdue for a vacation or just some simple, uninterrupted time in the evenings and weekends, it's time to give yourself a break. A well-rested soul is a healthy soul.

Rest Stop

1. How did you answer the question, "What do you do for leisure?"?

2. If you had more available time, what would you like to do for leisure?

3. Do you have a clear dividing line between your work and leisure time? If not, what steps might you take to protect that time?

4. How often do you take a vacation? If it has been a while, what is your excuse? When can you begin planning for a trip (with your husband or family) in the future?

THE ONE-WEEK DARE

Over the next week, I dare you to devote a half hour to one hour each day to leisure. Also, practice a Sabbath rest by refraining from work and other soul-draining activities for the entire weekend. Be sure to balance your leisure time between personal and family time. Do something you enjoy. Read a book. Start a new hobby. Go for a walk. Do something for *you*! For family leisure time, consider planning a movie night. Go on a picnic or a hike. Work on a family puzzle or play a board game. Begin a conversation with your kids about the things they would enjoy doing (personally and as a family) if you were to devote more time to leisure in your home. (Note: this may require removing some activities from the calendar to prioritize leisure.) Whatever you choose to engage in during your leisure time, make sure it is a type of leisure that is life-giving rather than soul-draining.

During this time (as well as on the weekends), I strongly encourage you to unplug from technology that takes up your time and saps your soul. Don't check e-mail. Don't get on social media. Those pictures and posts won't go anywhere. Don't feel obligated to check text messages or return them. In fact, turn off your phone or put it away while you are engaging in leisure time, and have the entire family follow suit. Do whatever it takes to reduce the distractions and model that leisure is an important and necessary discipline.

Bonus: For extra credit, plan a couple's vacation, family vacation, or a girls' trip. Set a date and pick a location. If it's a family vacation, involve everyone in the planning process. Even if it's a year away, it will give you something to look forward to.

Pay It Forward

Time for Others

It was a wonderful sermon. My pastor had encouraged the congregation to make a concentrated effort to reach out to our neighbors and actually get to know them. He went on to talk about how easy it is to get caught up in busyness and miss the needs around us. Busted. I felt an instant wave of conviction. At the end of the service, he introduced a campaign to get to know our neighbors in each of our respective neighborhoods. The assignment was simple: organize a gathering, which could be anything from a backyard barbecue to an ice-cream social. No strings attached. The main goal wasn't to invite them to church but simply to reach out and let them know we care.

To initiate the campaign, he had a giant map of the Austin area up on the stage and invited each family to come up and place a pin in their neighborhood to show their commitment to reach out to their neighbors. I immediately began to squirm as I thought of my calendar over the next several months. I had deadlines, travel, and other outside ministry obligations. Not to mention, I had put off several home-improvement projects due to my overcrowded schedule. My home was in no condition for a neighborhood gathering. Even if I could pull off the gathering, I had no time to nurture any connections we might make, which defeated the whole purpose of the outreach. While I was doing a mental inventory of all the cons, my husband leaned over and asked, "Should we go up?" Mind you, as a leader in the church, he feels a responsibility to participate in each and every outreach effort.

We ended up not committing to the outreach. The truth is God doesn't expect us to sign up for every outreach effort, and we were able to extend ourselves grace in regard to this particular one. However, it weighed heavily on my heart in the days that followed. I didn't feel conviction over not hosting a neighborhood gathering, but rather that my neighbors had become invisible to me, lost in the whirlwind of my frenzied, overcommitted life. And, truth be told, it wasn't just my neighbors. I was operating on fumes, with little left over to give to anyone, including my own family members.

Too Busy to Care

When it comes to caring for our neighbors, Jesus didn't beat around the bush. In Luke 10, He was asked by an expert in the Law (think seminary grad with an attitude), "Teacher, what shall I do to inherit eternal life?" (v. 25). Without hesitating, Jesus referred him back to the Shema (Deut. 6:5) and the Levitical Law (Lev. 19:18), which *every* teacher of the Law knew by heart. And then, just when you thought Jesus had humbled the teacher enough, the expert came back swinging. "Let's get specific, Jesus. If You want me to follow the Law, I need to know *exactly* whom I *have* to love. So who's my neighbor?" (my paraphrase, of course). As He often did, Jesus then told a story to make His point.

A man was traveling from Jerusalem to Jericho. To us, that's nothing more than a trip to Walmart. For anyone in the first century, though, the trip was treacherous. The seventeen-mile trek included a four-thousand-foot drop in elevation, over rough ground with crevasses, rocks, and caves (where bad guys liked to hang out so they could rob you on the way). In fact, that road is called "The Way of Blood" or "Bloody Pass" because of the danger from the terrain and the unsavory sorts who lay in wait.[1] Remember that; it's important.

Just as you'd think, the man got pummeled. Assaulted. Robbed and left for dead. Along came two different religious men—a priest and a Levite. Surely one of these holy men, these spiritually in-tune guys, would help. But no, the scripture says that the priest "passed by on the other side" (v. 31). A man who represented God to the people got as far away as possible from a person in need. Strike one for the religious. The Levite, a man who served in the temple, also saw the man, and taking a hint from the priest's playbook, crossed to the other side of the road and skedaddled. Strike two for the home team.

Remember, the Law commanded the people of God to care for each other. A Jewish man took better care of his animals than these two "holy" men took of a dying man. What made the first two men ignore an obvious need? Nobody knows. If the story were set in the twenty-first century, I'd chalk it up to overcrowded schedules and a fear of Ebola. What we do know is that somebody cared, and not the person anyone would suspect.

A Samaritan. (Insert collective gasp from Jesus' audience.)

Jews treated Samaritans like the scum of the earth. Worse than Gentiles. Lest you think I am referring to mild cultural prejudice here, let me set you straight. Some rabbis taught that a Jew was forbidden to help a Gentile woman who was in distress while giving birth. The reason? If the Gentile woman and her baby survived, one more Gentile had come into the world. Horrible, right? Well, the Jews thought Samaritans were even *worse*.[2]

Even though he had been treated worse than Gentiles, this Samaritan stopped to help the wounded man. Even though he could have been attacked, too, he refused to ignore the need staring him in the face. He stopped long enough to bandage "his wounds, pouring on olive oil and wine. Then he put him on his own animal, brought him to an inn, and took care of him" (v. 34 HCSB). His actions take up only one verse in the Bible, but they are grand gestures of grace and love. He took the time to bandage the wounds, which must have been severe—the man had been left to die. Slowing him down even more, the Samaritan saddled his donkey with the half-dead man and walked him all the way down that four-thousand-foot drop. The story ends with the man convalescing at an inn at the Samaritan's expense.

No, this is not a *real* story. It's a parable. It's meant to teach us important truths. Most of us have heard sermons about helping others in need. But how many of us have heard this parable used to teach the importance of *sacrificing our time* for the sake of others? In today's world we'd just call 911 and let someone else care for the man, with the justification that others are better qualified. And if we were in the wrong part of town, we'd leave before the ambulance got there. After all, the children are in the car. Truth is we don't want the interruption. Follow the ambulance to the hospital? Check him into the ER? Wait for his family to arrive—if he has any? Sit with him in the hospital room so he won't have to wake up in a strange place all alone? Um, no.

What I find interesting (and God-ordained) is the story that follows Jesus' telling of this parable. Are you ready for this? It focuses on the two sisters—Mary and Martha—and their two approaches to life. Yep. We've already learned so much from them, but seeing them in light of the parable of the good Samaritan brings both stories into such startling clarity. It's as if God knew that a bunch of women in the twenty-first century would struggle to rest and be still, so He put these two stories together. Can we see the connection? In one story, Jesus highlights the importance of noticing and paying attention to the needs around us, and in the very next breath, He highlights the plight of those who are too busy to be engaged in the present moment.

Perhaps the rush and fuss of our overcrowded lives blind us to the needs around us. We can't focus on the present moment (where needs always present themselves) because we're distracted by a million unimportant details, and by being so, we miss those God-appointed moments. We either miss those cues altogether or we purposely ignore them because we don't want to open up our schedules—or our hearts.

Honestly, when was the last time you paid enough attention to the needs right in front of you? When did you last take time out of your overbooked day to meet one of those needs? Or did you decide to let someone else help? Surely someone will come along soon. But for those lying half dead in the road, soon can be a very, very long time.

It's the Little Things

Did you notice what the Samaritan *didn't* do? He didn't open up a clinic for the needy. He didn't create a nonprofit foundation to address the prejudice between Jews and Samaritans. He saw a need. He met the need. End of story. How much good could Christendom accomplish if those who claimed to be Christ-followers followed the Samaritan's example? See need. Meet need. Go wash the dishes.

We live in an age of self-promotion, and while social media has connected us to the world in unimaginable ways, it has also hampered us from reaching out to that world with the love of Christ. Yes, we can post scriptures and show amazing Advent pictures, but in the same breath, we pause when we feel led to meet a need. Why? Because in comparison to other ministry activities we see posted on social media, our ordinary acts of service just don't seem, well, enough. Pictures of visiting orphanages in Eastern Europe. Blogs about blistered hands from building a well in Africa. Highlights from Christmas in Bethlehem complete with camels and yoked oxen. Who can compete with that? I know I'm not the only person who sees others' highlight reels and quietly dismisses her own anonymous kindness because it doesn't involve plane tickets, danger, or sleeping on the floor of a hut.

The early church didn't have to contend with unfettered access to information or else the gospel might not have been spread so effectively. Ironic, isn't it? While competition for headlines wasn't a struggle, the plights of comparison and recognition wormed their way into the minds of believers then, just as it does now:

> You are still worldly. For since there is jealousy and quarreling among you, are you not worldly? Are you not acting like mere humans? For when one says, "I follow Paul," and another, "I follow Apollos," are you not mere human beings?

What, after all, is Apollos? And what is Paul? Only servants, through whom you came to believe—as the Lord has assigned to each his task. I planted the seed, Apollos watered it, but God has been making it grow. So neither the one who plants nor the one who waters is anything, but only God, who makes things grow. The one who plants and the one who waters have one purpose, and they will each be rewarded according to their own labor. For we are co-workers in God's service; you are God's field, God's building. (1 Cor. 3:3–9 NIV)

The comparison game plagued the church at Corinth. Apparently both Paul and Apollos had ministered there, and apparently their personality and preaching styles created a bit of controversy. Who was the better minister? Who was more eloquent? Who was the better expositor of the Old Testament? Paul's response echoed his newly found passion for Christ. "Who cares about us? We're just servants of the Lord." The word *servants* is opposite of the word *masters* and was used for those of an inferior rank. Servants had no authority, no status, no prominence, and no power.[3] Paul turned prominence inside out and upside down. Rather than point out highlight reels of his church-planting efforts and applaud Apollos for his international traveling schedule, Paul reminded the church (and probably himself) that everybody plays a role in spreading the gospel—planting the seeds, pulling weeds, adding fertilizer, watering. No role gets the byline. Nobody's name gets listed first on the marquee. Only God gets the credit lines, and rightfully so.

I wonder if Paul would have a Facebook page if he were alive today.

Paul talked about little things—seeds and water. Both seem

boring. Trivial. Unimportant. Small. Especially in a world of supersized meals, birthday blowouts that require a small loan, and Starbucks Trenta coffees large enough to make an ox hyper. Listen, dear friend: God takes those seemingly small, unimportant, boring elements and transforms them. Loaves and fishes. Jars and torches. Locusts. A slingshot. Five smooth stones. A bush in the desert. Bread and wine.

As I'm writing this chapter, it's December. The season of pageants and holiday light tours and presents and malls and living nativities and ugly sweater contests. This month I also held my newborn grandson in my arms for the first time. Small. Frail. Fragile. Innocent. The stark contrast between the grandiosity of the holidays and the simple incarnation is unmistakable. God came to us in the smallest way possible. In a backwater town to nobody parents in a feeding trough that stunk of manure and hay and sweat. No doubt Mary wondered why God would use her, a pubescent girl. Joseph, just a carpenter. Both the unlikely of parents for the Son of God, King of kings, Prince of Peace. The shepherds must have marveled that angels would visit *them*. Stinky. Unclean. Unknown. Ordinary. Unimportant.

Yet the ordinary, unnoticed, and small are exactly what the world needs. A friend of mine noticed in her daughter's notebook a handwritten sign a friend had made. In bold letters, it said, "Go big or go home." That is our culture in a nutshell, but that is not how God operates. Ask your elderly neighbor. She doesn't need a reality-TV show to come build her a new house. She just wants some company. An errand run. A trip to the store. She wants to know she is not forgotten and not alone. Your child's teacher needs papers stapled and copies run. Your church staff needs to hear you say, "Thank you." The server at Sonic would appreciate a bigger tip when it's cold outside. The clerk bagging your groceries would readily accept your looking him in the eye, smiling, and saying, "I appreciate your help." That's probably not going to happen, though, if you are busy answering texts and "critical" e-mails while you're standing in line.

The problem is that you and I are running around at Mach 12 with our hair on fire, so we don't notice the small, ordinary gestures that make up the kingdom and change lives. Remember that old phrase, "If the devil can't make you bad, he'll make you busy"? Well played, ancient enemy, well played.

Everyone, a Minister

The story was all over the news. It all began when a customer in the drive-through line at a Starbucks in St. Petersburg, Florida, decided to "pay it forward" and buy coffee for the next person in line. The streak of kindness continued throughout the day for eleven hours, with 378 customers choosing to pay for the drink of a stranger in line behind them. Until, that is, customer #379 pulled up to the window to order a drink and, for reasons not disclosed, declined to extend the favor.[4]

I have to admit that when I first heard the story, I immediately passed judgment on customer #379, assuming he or she was a selfish, grouchy old curmudgeon. The truth is many of us are like customer #379 when it comes to paying it forward with the gospel. God bestowed His grace and forgiveness upon us as gifts. We did not earn them or, for that matter, even deserve them. There were no strings attached to the offer, but Jesus made it clear that He wanted us to pay it forward by sharing that same life-changing good news with others.

When we adopt an attitude of "go big or go home," we shirk our individual responsibilities to reach out to others in the love and name of Jesus. Busy mothers of preschoolers might reason, "I can't go on a two-week mission trip to the Congo." Others might rationalize, "I don't know how to open a homeless shelter or start a nonprofit." Since we can't go big, we stay home. This attitude (which all of us have had at one time or another) runs counter to Scripture:

> Therefore, if anyone is in Christ, he is a new creation. The old has passed away; behold, the new has come. All this is from God, who through Christ reconciled us to himself and gave us the ministry of reconciliation; that is, in Christ God was reconciling the world to himself, not counting their trespasses against them, and entrusting to us the message of reconciliation. Therefore, we are ambassadors for Christ, God making his appeal through us. We implore you on behalf of Christ, be reconciled to God. (2 Cor. 5:17–20)

Because I work with words for a living, I'm prone to notice how writers choose their words, including the writers of the Bible. Notice the little words Paul used in these verses. *Us* and *we*. Not *they* and *them*. Not *he* and *she*. We. Us. God uses *us*. All of us, not just evangelists or polished preachers. *We* are God's ambassadors. If that's intimidating, think of us as being messengers. Or think of witnesses to an event—how God has made all the difference in our lives. *That's* what we've been called to do. *That's* what our neighbors need to hear. *That's* what they need to see through our lives, in our actions.

When I was a new believer, I took evangelism-training classes. Four Spiritual Laws. The Roman Road. Evangelism Explosion. We learned how to make a cold call to somebody's door, share the gospel by going through several points and Bible verses we'd memorized, and encourage the unsuspecting homeowner to give her life to Jesus because she wasn't sure what she would say to God about why He should let her into heaven. While those techniques were effective in previous generations, today's culture is far too savvy, skeptical, skewed, and safety-conscious to allow such a conversation. However, few would reject a kind gesture that offers a bridge to future conversations about deep spiritual truths. Perhaps the best advice I learned in my vast assortment of evangelism training strategies was the simple truth, "People don't care how much you know until they know how much you care." And caring takes time.

In His last words to the disciples in Matthew's gospel, Jesus made this famous statement: "Go therefore and make disciples" (28:19). Go. Make disciples. Sounds intimidating. How does a mother of three preschool children make followers of Jesus? By loving those preschoolers and investing her time in them. By being honest and transparent with other mothers about her own struggles and the strength God has provided her. By being mindful in the present moment so she can hear God's gentle nudging to say a prayer, write a note of encouragement, or order takeout instead of cooking when her children need her undivided attention.

How does someone who juggles work and family manage to make followers of Jesus? By guarding what free time she has and refusing to overcommit to outside activities so she can be present and available to her family and coworkers. When we begin to see our children, coworkers, neighbors, and others with whom we come in contact on a consistent basis as a God-appointed ministry, rather than a burdensome obligation, we will, by default, want to make followers of Jesus. Our souls find their fulfillment and rest when we walk in obedience to our ultimate calling—to know Jesus and make Him known.

How that looks in your life will be dramatically different from your pastor's life. Or your husband's life. Or even your best friend's life. God has gifted you uniquely to make distinctly irreplaceable impressions on the lives of those you encounter, wherever you encounter them—at the grocery store or in the corporate office.

Although our gifts and spheres of influence are unique, one thing remains the same for all of us: we cannot give to others if we cannot notice a need. And we cannot notice a need if we have run ourselves into the ground. We won't want to care for others if we are burned out, used up, and worn thin.

First Things First

I've heard the preflight safety drill enough to have it practically memorized. Seat belts securely fastened. Check. Carry-on bags stored in the overhead bin or under the seat in front of me. Check. Emergency exits located in the front, the back, and over the wings. Check, check, check. By the time the flight attendant gets to the part about a loss in cabin pressure and oxygen masks deploying from above, I'm usually completely tuned out and engrossed in skimming through the SkyMall catalog or playing a game of solitaire on my tablet. However, on a recent flight, I snapped out of my trance when the flight attendant stopped by my row to tell the mother in the seat next to me with a young child in her lap to be sure to secure her own oxygen mask before placing a mask on her child. And that's when it struck me how very odd and out of character this action would be for a mother whose first concern in an emergency would likely be for her child.

One of the reasons I've saved this chapter for last is because I know there is a tendency among those of us who struggle with being overly busy, over-connected, and overwhelmed to take care of others before we take care of our own souls. Whether we are worn-out from a frenzied schedule, where we've put ourselves last on the list, or worn-out from ministerial service, the result is still the same. Unless we learn to take care of ourselves first, we will eventually find ourselves too incapacitated to care for others. When we breathe life into our souls by spending time with Christ, slowing down and taking time for physical rest as well as leisure, we are better equipped to help others. We will serve as a result of overflow rather than obligation. One of the greatest joys in life is to give to others what we have received for ourselves. However, we can't catch it on the run. We must learn to slow down and savor this beautiful gift God has given us.

As we come to a close with this intervention for our weary souls, the real work begins. Long-term change will require an attitude readjustment followed by drastic changes, but it will be well worth it in the end. However, we must individually decide for ourselves whether it's worth the fight. The time has come to decide.

I will end this book with the same challenge I issued in the introduction—a challenge God issued to the Israelite people in Jeremiah 6:16:

> "Stand at the crossroads and look;
>   ask for the ancient paths,
> ask where the good way is, and walk in it,
>   and you will find rest for your souls." (NIV)

Which path will you choose? Take it from a former weary soul, if you choose the good way, you will never look back. In that, you can rest assured.

Rest Stop

1. Can you recall an incident where you encountered a need and acted as the "good Samaritan"? If so, describe the encounter. Can you think of a time when you were too busy, too distracted, to meet a need brought to your attention? If so, describe what happened.

2. Can you think of a time when you were on the receiving end of a good Samaritan deed or an act of service? How did it make you feel?

3. On page 172, I mentioned that "the ordinary, unnoticed, and small are exactly what the world needs." How do you feel about that statement? Do you ever hesitate to serve because of the pervasive attitude of "go big or go home"?

4. Reread 2 Corinthians 5:17–20 and let it soak in. What did Christ give to us? What did He entrust to us? On a scale of 1 to 10, with 1 being "not so great" and 10 being "exceptional," how would you rank yourself when it comes to your performance as a "minister of reconciliation"?

If you are not satisfied with the number you put down, what steps might you take to improve in that area?

5. Is it difficult for you to tend to your own soul before serving others? What may be the reasons for that?

6. Do you currently serve others as a result of overflow or obligation? What are some steps you can take to change that if necessary?

THE ONE-WEEK DARE

Over the next week, I dare you to begin each morning by praying and asking God to make you aware of little ways you can bless someone's life during that day. Keep a blank journal to list the needs that come to your attention each day during the one-week period, and jot down how you met each need. If you're struggling to come up with ways to serve others, consider initiating one of the following ideas:

- Compliment a mom on how well-behaved her child is in a waiting room or checkout line.
- Put a few coins in an expired parking meter (if a car is next to it).
- Take donuts to work to share.
- Stop a gossip string at work (or church) by not listening or by not passing it along.
- Offer a homeless person your restaurant leftovers instead of taking them home.
- Let someone into your traffic lane.
- Write a former teacher to say thanks.
- Text a friend or coworker who has been sick or had a rough day to check on how she's doing.
- Compliment an elderly church member.
- Call your parents or grandparents.
- When you buy new clothes, donate some of your old ones.
- Donate old eyeglasses.

- Give someone else that prime parking spot.
- Make your husband's favorite dessert.
- Dog-sit.
- Babysit for a single parent.
- Make a point to thank every customer service person you encounter.
- Pay for the coffee of the person behind you in the coffee-shop drive-thru.
- Leave recent magazines or books in a doctor's waiting room.
- Leave your mail carrier cookies in your mailbox.
- Listen to others intently, maintaining eye contact.
- Accumulate your change and donate it to a charity.
- Compliment a stranger.
- Offer to help a friend pack up her belongings as she prepares to move.
- Drop off a vase of wildflowers on the porch of a friend who has had a rough day.
- Catch your child doing something right and praise him for it.
- Lend a pen to someone who needs one.
- Offer the repairman a glass of water.

A Thirty-Day Restoration Guide

The Thirty-Day Restoration Guide that follows is optional. Whether you are reading *Rest Assured* on your own or going through it with a group, this guide can be used when you are finished reading the book and upon completion of the four one-week dares, the recovery portion of Part 2. This guide offers a quick and simple overview of some of the key principles discussed throughout the book. If desired, it can be used as an accessory to your regular, daily time spent with God.

Day 1: Pray

Dear heavenly Father, as I begin this journey of reestablishing rest in my soul, I pray that You would reveal to me the enemies of rest that have invaded my life. I ask that You convict my heart to recognize that long-term change requires repentance rather than behavior

*modification. Help me understand that You created rest to
be a mandatory discipline rather than an optional luxury.
You set the example by modeling the importance of rest
throughout Your Word, beginning with the creation account
in which You rested on the seventh day. Help me examine
my heart and soul to uncover the reasons I avoid rest. Only
then will my soul be healed. Amen.*

Day 2: Claim

Read Jesus' invitation in Matthew 11:28–30 out loud, inserting
your name at the beginning of the passage.

> "[Your name], come to me, all who labor and are heavy
> laden, and I will give you rest. Take my yoke upon you,
> and learn from me, for I am gentle and lowly in heart,
> and you will find rest for your souls. For my yoke is easy,
> and my burden is light."

Now read the passage out loud in *The Message* translation:

> "Are you tired? Worn out? Burned out on religion? Come
> to me. Get away with me, and you'll recover your life.
> I'll show you how to take a real rest. Walk with me and
> work with me—watch how I do it. Learn the unforced
> rhythms of grace. I won't lay anything heavy or ill-fitting
> on you. Keep company with me and you'll learn to live
> freely and lightly."

Respond in prayer to Christ's invitation to rest.

Day 3: Reflect

I do believe in simplicity. It is astonishing as well as sad, how many trivial affairs even the wisest thinks he must attend to in a day; how singular an affair he thinks he must omit. When the mathematician would solve a difficult problem, he first frees the equation of all encumbrances, and reduces it to its simplest terms. So simplify the problem of life, distinguish the necessary and the real.

—HENRY DAVID THOREAU

What might your average day look like if you "reduced it to its simplest terms"?

Day 4: Reflect

And on the seventh day God finished his work that he had done, and he rested on the seventh day from all his work that he had done. So God blessed the seventh day and made it holy, because on it God rested from all his work that he had done in creation. (Gen. 2:2–3)

Ask yourself: Overall, have I done a good job of following God's established pattern of rest in my life? What are some examples that would support my belief?

Day 5: Ponder

We will not see lasting change until we admit that our chronic busyness is not the result of a scheduling problem, but rather a sin problem. Only a posture of sincere repentance will produce lasting change. (Chapter One)

What are your thoughts regarding this statement?

Day 6: Choose

Look over the list of "100 Ways to Give It a Rest" on pages 193–202 and choose one as your assignment for today.

Day 7: Declare

> "Be still, and know that I am God.
> I will be exalted among the nations,
> I will be exalted in the earth!" (Ps. 46:10)

The Hebrew word for "exalted" is *rûwm*, which means "to rise or raise; bring up, exalt; heave (up)."[1] God alone is to be exalted. He should be your primary affection. When you fail to pause and acknowledge that God alone is to be exalted, it is only a matter of time before you allow other things to steal your affection.

Ask yourself: In my failure to be still, what are some things I may have "exalted" or "heaved up" in my order of affections that have taken the place of God?

Day 8: Pray

Heavenly Father, help me cease striving and know You are God. I am tired of giving You my leftovers, and my soul aches to be closer to You. Give me strength to make the necessary changes. I am desperate to feel Your peace. Amen.

Day 9: Ponder

We live, in fact, in a world starved for solitude, silence, and private: and therefore starved for meditation and true friendship.

— C. S. LEWIS, *THE WEIGHT OF GLORY*

Ask yourself: How have technology and social media left me starved for meditation and true friendship?

Day 10: Ask Yourself

What do I crave more: to connect with God or to connect online? (Chapter Two)

Day 11: Reflect

"All things are lawful for me," but not all things are helpful. "All things are lawful for me, but I will not be dominated by anything." (1 Cor. 6:12)

Ask yourself: In what areas of my life has technology left me enslaved and mastered by a compulsion to engage?

Day 12: Respond

Think about the leisure activities you typically turn to when you have spare time and list them below. Go back and honestly appraise each one. Next to every activity, write either "soul-draining" or "life-giving." What changes might you need to make to engage in more healthy forms of leisure?

Day 13: Choose

Look over the list of "100 Ways to Give It a Rest" on pages 193–202 and choose one as your assignment for today.

Day 14: Pray

Heavenly Father, in this over-connected world of social media and unlimited information, my soul longs for true communion. Remind me that You wired my soul for this

*communion and that only You can completely satisfy my
soul's deepest longings. Help me purge my life of the things
that distract me from connecting with You. Amen.*

Day 15: Ponder

God can't give us peace and happiness apart from Himself
because there is no such thing.

—C. S. LEWIS

Day 16: Consider

Martha's striving to provide an exceptional meal caused her
to miss a truly exceptional experience. What if you took your
expectations down a notch and gave yourself permission to let go
of *exceptional* and make peace with *adequate*? (Chapter Three)

Day 17: Declare

Read this scripture for yourself out loud:

"Do not lay up for yourselves treasures on earth, where
moth and rust destroy and where thieves break in and
steal, but lay up for yourselves treasures in heaven, where
neither moth nor rust destroys and where thieves do not
break in and steal. For where your treasure is, there your
heart will be also." (Matt. 6:19–21)

Ask yourself: Where is my treasure?

Day 18: Ask Yourself

What has been my primary pursuit—the world's idea of the "good
life" or Jesus' promise of abundant life? What can I point to that
shows this is true?

Day 19: Reflect

God is far more concerned with our *holiness* than our *happiness*.
(Chapter Three)

Do you believe this statement to be true? Explain.

Day 20: Choose

Look over the list of "100 Ways to Give It a Rest" on pages 193–202
and choose one as your assignment for today.

Day 21: Pray

*Heavenly Father, in a culture that bombards me with
the message that happiness can be found in achievements,
wealth, possessions, pleasure, status, and children, it's hard
not to buy into the lie, and I find myself caught up in the
pursuit of happiness at some level. Help me recognize when
I begin to believe this lie. Remind me that You are the only
worthy pursuit. Amen.*

Day 22: Declare

I am at rest in God alone;
my salvation comes from Him.
He alone is my rock and my salvation,
my stronghold; I will never be shaken.
(Ps. 62:1–2 HCSB)

Day 23: Ponder

Worrying does not take away tomorrow's troubles; it takes away
today's peace.

—RANDY ARMSTRONG

Day 24: Declare

Write the following verse on a note card or save it as a note on your phone. Memorize the verse and save it for a difficult day.

> Even though . . .
>   yet I will rejoice in the LORD!
>   I will be joyful in the God of my salvation!
>   The Sovereign LORD is my strength! (Hab. 3:17,
>   18–19 NLT)

Day 25: Reflect

When we view God as an angry taskmaster who is more concerned with our behavior than our hearts, meeting with Him becomes more about maintaining the rules than maintaining the relationship. (Chapter Five)

Ask yourself: Is this my view of God?

Explain.

Day 26: Reflect

Only when our hearts are still and receptive can He unlock the mysteries of how He created us and then mold our identities according to His life-changing gospel of grace. Solitude allows us the time needed to marinate in His truths and define our identity according to who we are in Christ. Without solitude, we will strive and rush to conform to the world's preferences. (Chapter Six)

Record your thoughts about this statement.

Day 27: Choose

Look over the list of "100 Ways to Give It a Rest" on pages 193–202 and choose one as your assignment for today.

Day 28: Ponder

> Guard well your spare moments. They are like uncut diamonds. Discard them and their value will never be known. Improve them and they will become the brightest gems in a useful life.
>
> —RALPH WALDO EMERSON

Day 29: Reflect

Perhaps the rush and fuss of our overcrowded lives blinds us to the needs around us. We can't focus on the present moment (where needs always present themselves) because we're distracted by a million unimportant details, and by being so, we miss those God-appointed moments. We either miss those cues altogether or we purposely ignore them because we don't want to open up our schedules—or our hearts. (Chapter Eight)

Ask yourself: Is my life so busy and my schedule so crowded that I am left with no margin to see the needs around me and to care for others?

Explain.

Day 30: Pray

Heavenly Father, as this thirty-day restoration comes to a close, I pray that my commitment to rest will continue. Take these truths You have taught me and embed them deep within my heart. When I begin to stray off Your path of peace and rest again, convict my heart and help me respond immediately to the conviction and to repent with a godly sorrow. Thank You for Your patience and loving-kindness. Amen.

BONUS

100 Ways to Give It a Rest

Earth's crammed with heaven, and every common
bush afire with God. But only he who sees takes off his
shoes. The rest sit round it and pluck blackberries.

—ELIZABETH BARRETT BROWNING

1. Pick wildflowers and put them in tiny vases (baby food
   jars work great) around your house.
2. Watch a sunset in silence.
3. Sit on a porch swing with only your Bible and favorite
   beverage.
4. Spread out a blanket on the lawn underneath the stars on
   a clear evening; lie back, and enjoy the show.
5. Go on a hike and don't be in a hurry to get to a
   destination. Stop along the way to take in the elements of
   God's beautiful creation. Savor them.

6. Plant a fruit tree, nurture it, and enjoy the fruit of your labor.

7. Light candles around your house . . . just because.

8. Handwrite a letter to someone.

9. Make an anonymous donation to someone you know who is in need or send them a gift card for groceries.

10. Walk along an ocean beach by yourself. Take a small bag or tote with you and pick up seashells along the way. Repurpose them somewhere in your home. Not near a beach? Put that on your bucket list.

11. Take a weeklong break from snapping pictures of people with your phone. Instead, photograph only elements of nature. At the end of the week, upload your pictures into an album and thank God for the gifts you have often taken for granted.

12. Sit on your front or back porch and watch a storm come in. If you get a little wet, don't worry. You won't melt.

13. On a summer evening, go outside and find a place to sit and enjoy a cicada concert.

14. Build a sandcastle on the beach. Go ahead; be a kid again.

15. Hike to a creek, find a place to sit, and take in the creation around you.

16. Take a drive on a scenic county road. If you stumble upon a café or diner, go in and have a piece of pie.

17. Go into an antique store and buy an old book that catches your eye or has a contents page that looks interesting.

18. Be on the lookout for a bird's nest near your home. They are everywhere, but we often miss them in our busyness. If you can't find one, put up a birdhouse in your backyard.

19. Call family members for no reason other than to tell them you were thinking about them and love them.

20. When fall arrives and the leaves begin to drop, collect the colorful ones, put them in a wooden bowl or basket, and place the centerpiece somewhere in your home. (I do this every fall, and my kids make fun of me.)

21. Go wind chimes shopping. After listening to each one, buy the one that sounds the most pleasing to you. Hang it in a spot where you can most easily hear it in your home when the wind blows.

22. Pull up some classical music on iTunes or the Internet (Pandora radio is great for this.) and sample their music during the day while you work. Consider making a playlist of the tunes that touch your soul. (If you need to brush up on your classical composers, try out Vivaldi, Bach, Mozart, Chopin, Handel, Tchaikovsky, Beethoven, and Brahms.)

23. Gather up granola bars, peanut butter crackers, and other snack items in your pantry and put them in a bag in your car. When you come across a homeless person at an intersection, offer him or her some of the items.

24. Track down an old teacher (school or Sunday school), and write a note of appreciation for the investment he or she made in your life. Include a picture of your family. (If you can't think of a teacher, consider a neighbor, employer, or family member.)

25. Making s'mores by a campfire is a must at least once a year. Extra credit if you gather up a group of friends and ban all cell phones by the campfire.

26. Stop and smell the flowers. No, really, it's not just a saying. If you can't find any flowers to smell, buy some at

your local supermarket or farmers' market. No occasion. From you, to you, with love. You're worth it.

27. Get up early one morning while it's still dark; take a short walk and enjoy the silence.

28. Go into a craft store and pick up a puzzle. Work on it a little bit at a time.

29. Take a bubble bath.

30. Find a scenic trail and go on a bike ride (you can rent a cruiser bike if you don't have one). Go alone or invite a friend.

31. Go to a movie you've been wanting to see—all by yourself.

32. On a windy day, go to a park and fly a kite.

33. Find a nearby lake and rent a kayak for a few hours.

34. Plant an herb garden.

35. Pick a room in your house and organize it from top to bottom. It does your soul good to de-clutter your space.

36. Gather up a few treasured items from loved ones, such as your parents or grandparents who have passed on, and repurpose them into your home décor rather than keeping them tucked away.

37. Buy a wooden box at the craft store and create a blessing box. Put blank cards and a pen inside. Tell your family members to jot down blessings and answered prayers from time to time, date them, and put them in the box.

38. Plan a family picnic and play a game of kickball or Wiffle ball. (Don't keep score!)

39. Watch an old, classic movie. Popcorn and pj's are optional.

40. Buy a bird-watching book and a bird feeder, and learn more about the birds native to your area.

41. Create a playlist of all your favorite songs in middle and high school. Break it out when you clean house.

42. Grab a friend or your spouse and go out to eat at a restaurant that offers a quaint outdoor patio. Put your phones away for the entire meal.

43. Buy a magazine and thumb through it cover to cover.

44. If you have enough old pictures of your growing-up years scanned and saved digitally, design and purchase a photo book online. It will be fun to have them all in one place; your children and grandchildren will enjoy seeing the pictures.

45. Write down the story of how you became a Christian; include as much detail as possible. Your family members will want to have this on record for future generations.

46. Watch old home movies. If your kids are grown, consider inviting them over. If your kids are still young, show them movies of when they were first born.

47. Create an outdoor space where you can sit and enjoy nature. Add to it bit by bit each year. Include items like a comfy outdoor chair, a birdbath, wind chimes, a lantern, twinkle lights, and other soul-enriching elements.

48. Peruse a Goodwill store for a treasure to restore with a coat of chalk paint. (It can go on wood or metal with no prep.)

49. Clean out your master closet. If you haven't worn or used it in a year to eighteen months (shoes, handbags, clothes, outerwear), give it away for someone who will. Even though it's work, you'll feel better if you take steps to scale back and simplify your life.

50. Abstain from all technology for one solid day. Give your phone to someone you trust so you're not tempted to look at it. I promise you'll survive. Enjoy the silence.

51. Plan a dream vacation (for you and your spouse, for your family, or with friends) and keep a folder (hardcopy or online) of the details. Set a target date on the calendar and begin saving for it. After you determine how much you need, consider giving up something, such as lunch out or expensive coffee, and put the savings each month toward your vacation fund.

52. The next time a thunderstorm approaches, crack your windows open and enjoy the sounds and smells.

53. Plot out a half-mile course in your neighborhood and start walking. Try to walk three or four times a week. Not only is it good for your health, it's also good for your soul.

54. Put together a playlist of your favorite worship choruses. Begin each morning with music that ministers to your soul and ushers you into the presence of the Lord.

55. Set your phone alarm for 2:00 p.m. each day (or a time about halfway through your day). When your alarm goes off, stop what you're doing and think of three things you are grateful to God for providing.

56. Pick a month with thirty-one days and read a Proverb a day for that month. Highlight verses that speak to your heart.

57. Go to a craft store and pick up a beginner's kit for needlepoint, knitting, woodworking, painting, or another crafting hobby you've always wanted to try.

58. Visit an antique store and pick up a copy of a vintage magazine. Sit back and enjoy.

59. Make hot tea for yourself. Better yet, drink it out of a pretty china teacup.

60. Research your family tree online. Who knows, you may have someone famous in your lineage.

61. When fall arrives, gather up a bag of acorns on your next walk. When you get home, put them in a bowl of water. The ones that sink to the bottom have the most nutrients. Plant them (bottom down) in a planter on your back porch by tapping them into the top layer of rich soil about three to four inches apart (with the tops still exposed). Water them, and you just may have yourself an oak sapling in a few months. (Follow online directions for transplanting the sapling into your yard.)

62. Set up a coffee or dessert date with a friend you haven't seen in a while. Don't forget to put your phone away.

63. Find a mentor. Approach an older, wiser woman from your church or Bible study group and ask to meet one to two times a month to talk over coffee or lunch.

64. Find a friend who will swap childcare with you once a month so you can each take a "me day" to recharge your souls.

65. Google *hummingbird nest* and click on *images*. Check out the pictures. You'll thank me for this; I promise.

66. Choose a day and set your phone alarm to go off every three hours during the day. When it goes off, stop and touch base with God about your day. Be sure to thank Him for all His blessings. Before you know it, you will have developed a discipline of turning to Him all day.

67. Pull up the old classic hymns on your favorite Internet radio site and listen carefully to the lyrics.

68. One week, ask God to show you someone in your midst who has a need. Rather than rush through that week, be on the lookout for the need and meet it.

69. Spread out a blanket on your front lawn or at a park, lie back, and watch the people go by.

70. Play a board game with family or friends.

71. Rearrange the furniture in one of the rooms in your home.

72. Go to a park. If there's a swing set, go for it!

73. Set the DVR to record a movie or program you will enjoy sometime in the future.

74. Go shopping and spend some of the gift cards that have been sitting in your wallet unused.

75. Buy yourself a box of chocolates and reward yourself with one piece each day. You deserve it!

76. Make yourself or your family a big breakfast. If you're used to eating breakfast on the run, start a new tradition. The smell of bacon will brighten anyone's day.

77. Organize the junk drawer in your house or garage.

78. Gather up a group of close friends and go country and western dancing. If you don't know how, just observe until you catch on. It's easy!

79. Plant a butterfly garden (look online for instructions) and create a habitat for some of God's most beautiful creatures.

80. Stare out the window for two minutes and take in the sights you normally take for granted.

81. Be on the lookout for a heart-shaped rock. Pick it up and put it somewhere in your home to remind you of God's unfailing love. (I have clusters of them all over my house!)

82. Buy yourself a new pillow for your bed—and make sure it's a nice one. Considering how much time you spend using it, it is a justified purchase. Besides, everyone deserves a favorite pillow.

83. Select a Bible verse you'd like to memorize, write it on a card, and tape it to your bathroom mirror. Put another copy in your car and another in your purse.

84. Visit a local feed store to see, and maybe even hold, baby chicks.

85. Change your hairstyle or try a new hair color.

86. The next time you're at the store, buy a pint of your favorite ice cream. You know, the one you usually avoid because of the high calorie count. Take a bite here and there for a snack and savor it over a long period of time. Your thighs can handle it, in moderation.

87. Visit a nearby vineyard for a wine tasting.

88. During the Christmas holidays, pack up everyone in the car and take a drive to that neighborhood with the awesome Christmas lights. Take along hot cocoa in thermal mugs.

89. Visit a museum in your city or a nearby community. Lots of museums offer free or reduced-price tickets on certain days.

90. Hang up a hummingbird feeder and wait for them to buzz by for a visit. Be patient—it may take a while for the hummingbirds to arrive. They enjoy the warmer months. Be sure to change out the nectar on a regular basis.

91. Gather a group of your friends and go hear a live band. Perhaps you can find tickets for a concert featuring a group from your high school or college days.

92. Buy a new journal and keep it by your Bible. When God uses a particular verse to speak to your heart, write it down in your journal and put a date next to it.

93. Plant tulip bulbs in the fall and behold their beauty in the spring.

94. Ride a roller coaster. Be a kid again and throw your arms in the air and scream your head off.

95. Pick wildflowers and press them between the pages of a book.

96. The next time you see a rainbow, stop and take it in.

97. Skip rocks on a lake or pond.

98. Collect pretty rocks, minerals, fossils, old vintage glass, petrified wood, and other treasures; save them in a glass jar and put them on display in your home.

99. Make a snowman. No snow where you live? Put that on your bucket list too.

100. Begin your own personal list of one hundred life moments you want to enjoy; add to it as you experience small moments that enrich your soul. Refer to it when your soul needs a boost.

Acknowledgments

To my husband, Keith: Thank you for picking up the slack when the collateral damage from my frenzied pace would spill over into our family life. When I was tempted to say yes to too much, you often stepped in and said no. In doing so, you fought for our family and, more important, my soul. Thank you for being the spiritual leader God called you to be. Now that much of the chaos has subsided (translation: the children have flown the nest), I am so grateful we invested in our relationship over the years, despite the often-times hectic pace. You fought for our regular date nights and made sure our marriage was a priority. I'm looking forward to perfecting this rest thing in the years to come with my very best friend by my side.

To my three grown children and the bonus children I gained when you married (Ryan and Casey, Paige and Matt, Hayden and Becca): Spending time with you guys is my favorite form of leisure. Not a day goes by that I'm not thankful for the fact that we all truly enjoy one another's company. Spending time with family is one of the greatest joys in my life. You guys are good for my soul.

To my two precious grandsons, Walker and Micah: Thank you for teaching Mimi how to do life more slowly. You have reminded me that the little things are really the big things.

To my counselor, Chris Thurman: I can still remember working up my courage to schedule that first appointment several years ago. Making that phone call was a first step in admitting that my soul was on life support. Thank you for helping me parse through the fallout and, more importantly, reconnect with the only One who could nurture my soul back to health. I am forever grateful for your guidance and your friendship.

To Siobhan and Becky: One of the greatest blessings in my newly balanced life is reconnecting with my two college roomies—maids of honor in my wedding! It's a shame that we let nearly three decades go by before getting together. When we reconnected over breakfast last year, it was as if we had never been apart. We laughed. We cried. We reminisced. And we marveled at the bikini pics I brought from our college days and laughed some more. As I drove away from that breakfast, I realized how much I have missed you two and vowed to make sure we never lose touch again. I'm looking forward to making up for lost time.

To my go-to gal at W Publishing, Debbie Wickwire: You are a breath of fresh air. When I fell off the "rest wagon" while writing this book, your encouragement to write from that place was just the nudge I needed. It reminded me of a quote I once read by Augustine:

> WE, WHO PREACH AND WRITE BOOKS. . . . WRITE WHILE WE MAKE PROGRESS. WE LEARN SOMETHING NEW EVERY DAY. WE DICTATE AT THE SAME TIME AS WE EXPLORE. WE SPEAK AS WE STILL KNOCK FOR UNDERSTANDING.

Amen to that. Thank you for encouraging me to write while I still knock for understanding.

And, finally, to the Great Shepherd who is in the business of restoring souls: You alone are the never-ending source of life and peace. Thank You for being patient when I forget that truth and scramble down another path in search of something else to still my restless soul. Point me back to the "good way" and help me walk in it.

Notes

Introduction

1. Matthew Henry, *Matthew Henry's Commentary on the Whole Bible: Complete and Unabridged in One Volume* (Matthew 11:25–30) (Peabody, MA: Hendrickson, 1996).

Chapter One: The Badge of Busyness

1. James Strong, *A Concise Dictionary of the Words in the Greek Testament and the Hebrew Bible* (Bellingham, WA: Logos Research Systems, Inc., 2009), s.v. "*râphâh.*"
2. Ibid., s.v. "*shâbath.*"
3. John Ortberg, *The Life You've Always Wanted: Spiritual Disciplines for Ordinary People* (Grand Rapids, MI: Zondervan, 2004), 79.
4. Richard A. Swenson, MD, *Margin: Restoring Emotional, Physical, Financial, and Time Reserves to Overloaded Lives* (Colorado Spring, CO: NavPress, 2004), 69.
5. Bronnie Ware, *The Top Five Regrets of the Dying* (Carlsbad, CA: Hay House, 2012), quoted in Susie Steiner, "The 5 Things People Regret Most on Their Deathbed," *The Guardian*, December 5, 2013.
6. Kevin DeYoung, *Crazy Busy: A (Mercifully) Short Book about a (Really) Big Problem* (Wheaton, IL: Crossway, 2013); Kindle version: Location 664 of 1345.

7. Strong, *A Concise Dictionary*, s.v. "*mĕtanŏĕō*."

Chapter Two: The Exhausting Pursuit of Happiness

1. Mrs. Van Koert Schuyler, "Living Beyond Their Strength," *Ladies' Home Journal*, September 1894, 4.

2. Ibid.

3. "Is There a Difference between Joy and Happiness?" accessed August 21, 2014, http://www.gotquestions.org/joy-happiness .html#ixzz3DhMTPSCN.

4. James Strong, *A Concise Dictionary of the Words in the Greek Testament and the Hebrew Bible* (Bellingham, WA: Logos Research Systems, Inc., 2009), s.v. "*gûwl*."

5. Mrs. Margaret Bottome, "The King's Daughters," *Ladies' Home Journal*, April 1896, 26.

6. Strong, *A Concise Dictionary*, s.v. "*pŏlus*."

7. H. D. M. Spence-Jones, ed. *The Pulpit Commentary: St. Luke* (Bellingham, WA: Logos Research Systems, Inc., 2004), 277.

8. Matthew Henry, *Matthew Henry's Commentary on the Whole Bible: Complete and Unabridged in One Volume* (Luke 10:38–42) (Peabody, MA: Hendrickson, 1996).

9. Juliet B. Schor, "The Overspent American: Upscaling, Downshifting, and the New Consumer," *The New York Times on the Web*, http://www.nytimes.com/books/first/s/schor-overspent.html.

10. Merriam-Webster.com, s.v. "conspicuous consumption," accessed July 31, 2014, http://www.merriam-webster.com/dictionary /conspicuous%20consumption.

11. Thorstein Veblen, *The Theory of the Leisure Class: An Economic Study of Institutions* (New York: McMillian & Co., 1899), 84.

12. Alice Bartram, "When There Is a Surplus," *Ladies' Home Journal*, September 1894, 4.

13. Ibid.

14. R. A. Clay, "Stressed in America," *American Psychological Association*, January 2011, vol. 42, no. 1, accessed August 2, 2014, http://www.apa.org/monitor/2011/01/stressed-america.aspx.

15. Strong, *A Concise Dictionary*, s.v. "*ophthalmos*."

16. Brainyquote.com, accessed August 3, 2014, http://www .brainyquote.com/quotes/quotes/h/henrydavid153913 .html#FBvsXfSuUSPuO78f.99.

17. Robert Frank, "Millionaire Says Money 'Prevents Happiness,'" *Wall Street Journal*, February 9, 2010, http://blogs.wsj.com /wealth/2010/02/09/millionaire-says-money-prevents-happiness/.

18. Aristotle, in *The Nicomachean Ethics*, ed. Lesley Brown, trans. David Ross (New York: Oxford University Press; July 15, 2009); Kindle version: Location 140 of 6858.

19. Strong, *A Concise Dictionary*, s.v. "*pĕrissŏs*."

20. Ibid., s.v. "*zētĕō*."

21. Matthew Henry, *Matthew Henry's Commentary on the Whole Bible: Complete and Unabridged in One Volume* (Col. 3:1–4) (Peabody, MA: Hendrickson, 1996).

22. Strong, *A Concise Dictionary*, s.v. "*phrŏnĕō*."

23. J. F. Walvoord and R. B. Zuck, *The Bible Knowledge Commentary: An Exposition of the Scriptures*, vol. 2 (Wheaton, IL: Victor Books, 1983), 680.

24. James Strong, *A Concise Dictionary of the Words in the Greek Testament and the Hebrew Bible* (Bellingham, WA: Logos Research Systems, Inc., 2009), s.v. "*mĕtanŏĕō*."

Chapter Three: Tethered Souls

1. Jessica Bennett, "Bubbles Carry a Lot of Weight: Texting Anxiety Caused by Little Bubbles," *The New York Times*, August 29, 2014,

http://www.nytimes.com/2014/08/31/fashion/texting-anxiety
-caused-by-little-bubbles.html?_r=0.

2. David Bendel Hertz, "Cybernetics," *Seventeen Magazine*, October 1949, 114–15.

3. Sara Perez, "iTunes App Store Now Has 1.2 Million Apps, Has Seen 75 Billion Downloads to Date," *Tech Crunch*, June 2, 2014, http://techcrunch.com/2014/06/02/itunes-app-store-now-has-1–2 -million-apps-has-seen-75-billion-downloads-to-date/.

4. Richard A. Swenson, MD, *In Search of Balance: Keys to a Stable Life* (Colorado Springs, CO: NavPress, 2010), 32.

5. Ibid.

6. Maria Konnikova, "How Facebook Makes Us Unhappy," *The New Yorker*, September 10, 2013, http://www.newyorker.com/tech /elements/how-facebook-makes-us-unhappy.

7. Kevin DeYoung, *Crazy Busy: A (Mercifully) Short Book about a (Really) Big Problem* (Wheaton, IL: Crossway, 2013); Kindle version: Location 892 of 1345.

8. Strong, *A Concise Dictionary*, s.v. "*mĕtanŏĕō.*"

Chapter Four: Worried Sick

1. David Ropeik, "How Risky Is It, Really? Why Our Fears Don't Always Match the Facts," *Psychology Today*, December 27, 2011, http://www.psychologytoday.com/blog/how-risky-is-it-really/201112 /time-worry-about-worrying-too-much.

2. Centers for Disease Control and Prevention, s.v. "*Naegleria fowleri,*" accessed December 1, 2014, http://www.cdc.gov/parasites/naegleria/.

3. National Weather Services, "How Dangerous Is Lightning?" accessed May 4, 2014, http://www.lightningsafety.noaa.gov/odds.htm.

4. "Bee Sting Facts," accessed May 4, 2014, http://www .buzzaboutbees.net/bee-sting-facts.html.

5. "Dog Bite Fatalities," accessed May 4, 2014, http://www.dogsbite
.org/dog-bite-statistics-fatalities.php.

6. *Goodreads*, s.v. "worrying," accessed April 5, 2014, http://www
.goodreads.com/quotes/612549-worrying-does-not-take-away
-tomorrow-s-troubles-it-takes-away.

7. J. P. Louw, J. P. Nida, and E. A. Nida, eds. *Greek-English Lexicon of
the New Testament: Based on Semantic Domains* (New York: United
Bible Societies, 1996), s.v. "*ĕpirrhiptō.*"

8. James Strong, *A Concise Dictionary of the Words in the Greek
Testament and the Hebrew Bible* (Bellingham, WA: Logos Research
Systems, Inc., 2009), s.v. "*tarassō.*"

9. Strong, *A Concise Dictionary*, s.v. "*ĕirēnē.*"

10. John F. Walvoord and Roy B. Zuck, eds. *The Bible Knowledge
Commentary: An Exposition of the Scriptures* (Wheaton, IL: Victor
Books, 1983), s.v. "Habakkuk 3:17."

11. Oswald Chambers, *My Utmost for His Highest*, July 16
(Uhrichsville, OH: Barbour Publishing, Inc., 2000).

12. Strong, *A Concise Dictionary*, s.v. "*mĕtanŏĕō.*"

Chapter Five: Prioritize the One Thing Needed

1. James Strong, *A Concise Dictionary of the Words in the Greek
Testament and the Hebrew Bible* (Bellingham, WA: Logos Research
Systems, Inc., 2009), s.v. "*pĕrispaō.*"

2. Matthew Henry, *Matthew Henry's Commentary on the Whole
Bible: Complete and Unabridged in One Volume* (Luke 10:38–42)
(Peabody, MA: Hendrickson, 1996).

3. H. D. M. Spence-Jones, ed. *The Pulpit Commentary: St. Mark
Vol. 1* (Bellingham, WA: Logos Research Systems, Inc.,
2004), 7.

4. Strong, *A Concise Dictionary*, s.v. "*parrhēsia.*"

Chapter Six: Create Room to Breathe

1. Matthew Henry, *Matthew Henry's Commentary on the Whole Bible: Complete and Unabridged in One Volume* (Psalm 23) (Bellingham, WA: Logos Research Systems, Inc., 2005).

2. James Strong, *A Concise Dictionary of the Words in the Greek Testament and the Hebrew Bible* (Bellingham, WA: Logos Research Systems, Inc., 2009), s.v. "*shûwb.*"

3. Ibid., s.v. "*anapauō.*"

4. Matthew Henry, *Matthew Henry's Commentary on the Whole Bible: Complete and Unabridged in One Volume* (Mark 6:32) (Bellingham, WA: Logos Research Systems, Inc., 2005).

5. Ibid.

6. Mrs. Van Koert Schuyler, "Living Beyond Their Strength," *Ladies' Home Journal*, September 1894, 4.

7. Ibid.

8. Henri Nouwen, in *The Essential Henri Nouwen*, ed. Robert A. Jonas (Boston: Shambhala, 2009), 100.

9. Charles Swindoll, *Intimacy with the Almighty: Encountering Christ in the Secret Places of Your Life* (Nashville: J. Countryman, 1999), 280.

10. Ralph Waldo Emerson, BrainyQuote.com, accessed March 17, 2014, BrainyQuote.com, http://www.brainyquote.com/quotes /quotes/r/ralphwaldo103415.html.

Chapter Seven: Give Yourself a Break

1. Dictionary.com, http://dictionary.reference.com/browse/leisure.

2. Bureau of Labor Statistics, "American Time Use Survey," accessed February 27, 2014, http://www.bls.gov/tus/charts/leisure.htm.

3. Pulpit Commentary, *Bible Hub*, s.v. "Ephesians 5:11," accessed April 2, 2014, http://biblehub.com/commentaries/pulpit /ephesians/5.htm.

4. Daily Mail Reporter, "How smartphones and tablets are adding Two Hours to our working day," October 30, 2012, http://www.dailymail.co.uk/sciencetech/article-2225325/Smartphones-tablets-add-TWO-HOURS-working-day.html.

5. William Bigelow, "Study: Workers with Smartphones at Health Risk," *Breitbart*, September 24, 2014, http://www.breitbart.com/national-security/2014/09/24/german-study-workers-with-smartphones-at-health-risk/.

6. Ben Spencer, "Checking Work Email at Home Can Cause Heart Problems, Anxiety and Headaches Warn Experts," *Daily Mail*, September 23, 2014, http://www.dailymail.co.uk/health/article-2766714/Checking-work-email-home-cause-heart-problems-anxiety-headaches-warn-experts.html.

7. Sharona Schwartz, "How Farmers in Israel Are Preparing for a Rare Biblical Event That Starts This Week," *The Blaze*, September 24, 2014, http://www.theblaze.com/stories/2014/09/24/how-farmers-in-israel-are-preparing-for-a-rare-biblical-event-that-starts-this-week/.

8. Arianna Huffington, "40 Percent of American Workers Will Leave Paid Vacation Days Unused," *Huffington Post*, August 19, 2014, http://www.huffingtonpost.com/arianna-huffington/paid-vacation-days_b_5693225.html.

9. James Strong, *A Concise Dictionary of the Words in the Greek Testament and the Hebrew Bible* (Bellingham, WA: Logos Research Systems, Inc., 2009), s.v "akal."

10. "Give Yourself a Break Today," *WebMD*, accessed September 2, 2014, http://www.webmd.com/balance/features/take-a-break.

Chapter Eight: Pay It Forward

1. IVP New Testament Commentaries, "Discipleship: Looking to Our Neighbor, to Jesus and to God," accessed November 11, 2014,

https://www.biblegateway.com/resources/commentaries/IVP-NT
/Luke/Discipleship-Looking-Our-Jesus.

2. David Guzik Commentary, "Study Guide for Luke 10," *Blue Letter Bible*, 2000, accessed November 12, 2014, http://www.blueletterbible.org/Comm/guzik_david/StudyGuide_Luk/Luk_10.cfm?a=983029.

3. Barnes' Notes on the Bible, s.v. "1 Corinthians 3:5," *Bible Hub*, accessed November 12, 2014, biblehub.com/commentaries/1_corinthians/3-5.htm.

4. Paulina Firozi, "378 People 'Pay It Forward' at Starbucks," *USA Today Network*, August 21, 2014, http://www.usatoday.com/story/news/nation-now/2014/08/21/378-people-pay-it-forward-at-fla-starbucks/14380109/.

A Thirty-Day Restoration Guide

1. James Strong, *A Concise Dictionary of the Words in the Greek Testament and the Hebrew Bible* (Bellingham, WA: Logos Research Systems, Inc., 2009), s.v. "*rûwm*."

About the Author

Vicki Courtney is a national speaker and the bestselling author of numerous books and Bible studies, including *Move On*, *Ever After*, *5 Conversations You Must Have with Your Daughter*, and *5 Conversations You Must Have with Your Son*. Vicki is a past ECPA Christian Book Award recipient in the Children and Youth category. She and her husband have three grown children, a son-in-love, two daughters-in-love, and two amazing grandsons.